# A Drop of Grace

## Finding and Protecting our Common Ground

Prudence Foster



ISBN: 978-1-7353772-0-9

# DEDICATION

For Augie, Dakota and Michael

# CONTENTS

# PROLOGUE

The title of this book, *A Drop of Grace*, can be interpreted in a number of ways. First and foremost, it is meant to capture the idea that in order to solve the world's growing environmental problems, we're most likely to succeed if we have a measure of grace in how we approach this discussion. A generous dollop of open-mindedness, kindness, and love. If we are respectful of one another's viewpoints, and are sincerely eager to learn what others have to say, we will be able to hear others. In turn, we are more likely to be heard. When we acknowledge that each person has wisdom, however different that may be from our own, we can usually uncover common goals and values. The civility of graciousness grants us access to each other's insights and promotes a willingness to work together. This respect is essential for resolving the modern day crises we have created.

*A Drop of Grace* is also intended to represent the fact that each of us leaves a material footprint on this earth through our day-to-day living. We buy goods and services, we walk and eat, and we dispose of trash and burn fuels. All our activities impact natural ecosystems. The choices we make, when multiplied by the 7 billion people on the planet, are having a dramatic impact on the natural world. Our droplets of impact are pooling up, resulting in the dramatic depletion and pollution of our global natural resources. We can ask the question "Is my individual droplet a life affirming one or a resource heavy - pesticide ridden - plastic laden - heavy metal polluted one?" At the very least, aren't we all morally responsible for the composition of our individual droplets?

Finally, the title is meant to convey the idea that one drop of grace may act as a catalyst and spark a sea of change. Any one of our actions may be the one which tips the balance and triggers an important change in the way an industry makes its products, in the policies a government enacts, or in the choices our neighbors make. Each of our environmentally friendly choices sends out ripples in the economic, governmental, and social spheres not to forget improving the ecological impacts of our own droplets. What message do our droplets send?

It is with a deep yearning to protect the stunningly beautiful natural world that I write this book. I hope to explain why I think environmental issues are so very important. Not so I can convince you 'I know best'. But that others might come to understand and respect that 'protecting the environment is best for all of us' is a valid viewpoint. I hope to strengthen our recognition that nature is, quite literally, our common ground. Ecological well-being is of uncountable benefit to us all. The conservation of wilderness is a moral imperative from many angles: the preservation of species, alleviation of poverty, and the welfare of future generations.

Most wonderfully, ecologically-minded lifestyle choices are also capable of reframing our relationship with capitalism as we prioritize non-monetary forms of wealth such as health, social relationships, and skill sets. With humility, I hope that we may all find more grace in our lives and celebrate the common ground we share with one another.

# 1 COMMON GROUND

These days, distrust between people of different points of view seems to be rampant. This distrust is so pronounced that it is inhibiting our ability to progress on many issues. I believe our best way through this is to respect one another's wisdom and to endeavor to find common ground. Call it grace; call it open-mindedness. Whatever you call it, the need for mutual civility has never been greater. It seems to me that divisions in our culture are getting stronger day by day, that we are finding it more difficult to understand the perspective of people outside our own bubbles.

In these pages, I shall endeavor to present why environmental issues are moral imperatives, urgent, and everyone's responsibility. But fear not, it is not so difficult to be environmentally conscious. It is mostly about a shift in perception, which can have profound and wonderful ramifications for the quality of our lives. This book is the culmination of a lifetime of thinking about how to protect nature on our glorious planet. It is my obsession. All my life, I've been concerned about making space for other species - from saving earthworms on the pavement to being actively involved in environmental volunteering right through to an academic career studying natural global cycles.

I hope to convince you that eco-conscious living is essential for humanity's health and survival, integral to achieving social and intergenerational justice, and an opportunity to shift our culture away from materialism, rising mental illnesses, and work-dominance. On the flip side, I'll explain why eco-conscious living enables more life-affirming behaviors and greater social, resource, and food security. I'll argue that eco-conscious living is also vital for our and future generations' mental, physical, and spiritual health while also addressing global issues of wealth inequality and corruption. As you may have gathered, I see eco-consciousness as a moral imperative. It has always puzzled me that it is not *visibly* fundamental to the operation of the world's religions. In particular, environmentalism and Christianity are not diametrically opposed value systems, despite what some politicians would lead us to believe. In fact, at their cores, the two systems share a vast river of common values: community, poverty alleviation, and social justice, as manifested by the existence of many environmentally oriented Christian organisations. And it is not just Christianity which touches on the sanctity of the natural world, all the world's major religions do so.[1, 2]

Let me firmly state at the outset that I'm not trying to induce guilt or to try and change your values or to add things to your to-do list. Instead, I'm trying to explain where my environmentalism comes from, and how dire the state of the planet really is. After 35 years of environmental concern, I have come to believe that it is our individual actions which are the key levers to effecting the change necessary for humans to survive and thrive, for there to be wealth equality, and intergenerational justice.

I will not demand that "You should" or "You shouldn't" do such and such, rather I will focus on the what, the how, and why of environmental depletion. Then you will be enabled to choose if you wish to pursue more eco-conscious choices or to be more supportive of ongoing eco-efforts. Just as my own reactions to Christianity were transformed by learning to love a mid-western Christian family, perhaps your reactions to environmentalism will be changed by reading this book, as. I know my own eco-practices have been changed by the research for this book. And I also want to share the positive sides of adopting eco-conscious habits and impart hope about the future. There are many clever solutions out there and many many people and organizations working on solving our environmental woes. Together, we can make the world a safer, more bountiful, and even more beautiful place.

---

[1] Reuter, T.A. 2015, "The green revolution in the World's Religions: Indonesian examples in international comparison", Religions 6, 1217-1231, https://doi.org/10.3390/rel6041217

[2] The Forum on Religion and Ecology at Yale, fore.yale.edu

I'll be covering a lot of ground in this book. In Chapter 2, I identify 8 key natural resources upon which human life depends. I then discuss the status of these 8 resources from a variety of angles so we can get an overall picture of the state of the natural world rather than a one-off study targeting one ecosystem for example. The overall depleted state of the planet is quite alarming. Chapter 3 discusses what is driving this depletion – is it transportation or food? The clothing or health product industry? In Chapter 4, I discuss what we can do to nurture our natural resources and conclude that it's essential that we, as individual consumers, change how and what we buy. In Chapter 5, I explore the positive benefits to ourselves and to society of adopting some of these eco-conscious behaviors. In Chapter 6, I explore some of the reasons we tend to give for not changing our behaviors to healthier ones. I developed an eco-denial spectrum in writing that chapter and found it interesting to notice how I borrow reasons for inaction from different categories at different times. The final chapter concludes with reasons for hope – and be assured there are many.

This introductory chapter is a personal appeal to the reader to consider these issues, and as such, it is also an appeal to trust me. I, therefore, lay open some of my own story. Developing eco-conscious behaviors is a deeply personal journey, and so I thank you for being brave enough, inspired enough, or curious enough to engage with my thoughts on the subject. Our first step on this journey is to find a common starting point.

## Protecting nature as common ground

Humor me for a moment. Take a deep breath and pause. Rest. Bring to mind a favorite memory of the outdoors. Maybe even close your eyes.

Have you got a particular moment in mind? Perhaps you share one of mine: the pungent smells and vivid colors of autumn, the clean sharp air of winter and a sparkling winter sky, a brimming wildflower meadow, an elemental day at the beach, a hike in the mountains ... I want to stay nestled in these thoughts. What do those memories mean to you? Which aspect of the scene is strongest? Scent or color? The temperature or the breeze? The scenery? For me, these thoughts are powerfully evocative. When I'm outdoors I often experience powerful upwellings of love, goodwill, delight, and peace. Sometimes a place will fling me into a childhood memory such as the delight my siblings and I had as children when we found a lady slipper in the woods - our mom's favorite flower, or when as teenagers we stood on the beach looking for shooting stars. I connect instantly to those moments.

I think almost all of us experience nature with a sense of wonder and awe. Indeed, on my spiritual journey, the transcendental emotions I experience when I'm in a place of great natural beauty are what first opened me up to the possibility of a creator. Many religions touch on the sacredness of the natural world either as a manifestation of the creator or as his or her creation which is to be cherished, nurtured, and protected. Perhaps we all deeply desire the conservation of the wilderness and feel sadness at the loss of species, rich soil, and ecosystems, clean free-flowing rivers or rolling oceans. But it does not necessarily follow that all of us regard it as a moral imperative to protect the environment.

Nonetheless, I think many or perhaps most of us would agree that sharing our wealth, feeding the hungry and alleviating suffering are moral imperatives. In order to secure clean water, food, and security for people everywhere, we need to protect our natural resources. It is obvious that we all rely on fresh air, fresh water, and vibrant soils for our well being. But we also rely on healthy ecosystems and wilderness. For it is in healthy ecosystems that air and water are cleansed and regulated, that pollinators live and breed, and so on.

We are already suffering from environmental degradation with an estimated 13 million deaths a year attributed to poor environmental factors. The poor are disproportionately dependent on healthy environments with 36% of the total wealth of low-income countries estimated to come directly from natural capital. In addition, 70% of those who live below the poverty line depend directly on natural resources for their livelihoods. It is, in part, because of these links between the environment and alleviating poverty that development strategies now consider the two issues as inseparable.[3]

Therefore, if we view alleviating poverty as a moral imperative, then protecting our natural resources is also a moral imperative. And of course, as resource consumption continues to increase, future generations will suffer much more than we are suffering today on account of this ongoing environmental degradation. The link between today's consumption and tomorrow's hunger, poverty, and strife is part of intergenerational justice and is another reason why it is a moral imperative to protect the environment. World leaders, including the UN Secretaries-General Ban Ki-moon and António Guterres[4] concur with this sentiment. Pope Francis often discusses the moral imperative to protect creation, for instance:

> *"The human family has received from the Creator a common gift: nature. The Christian view of creation includes .... wisely using resources for the benefit of all, with respect for the beauty, finality and usefulness of every living being and its place in the ecosystem. Nature, in a word, is at our disposition and we are called to exercise a responsible stewardship over it. Yet so often we are driven by greed and by the arrogance of dominion, possession, manipulation and exploitation; we do not preserve nature; nor do we respect it or consider it a gracious gift which we must care for and set at the service of our brothers and sisters, including future generations."* [5]

It is a great sadness to me that the protection of the natural world has become a burden and even more so that it is used politically to divide conservatives and liberals. In the history of the

---

[3] UNDP-UNEP 2015, "Mainstreaming Environment and Climate for Poverty Reduction and Sustainable Development: A Handbook to Strengthen Planning and Budgeting Processes", available at www.unpei.org

[4] https://www.un.org/press/en/2015/sgsm16710.doc.htm accessed November 12, 2019

[5] https://www.cacatholic.org/policies-issues/human-dignity/care-creation/quotes-pope-francis-creation accessed November 12, 2019

United States, for example, it has been Republicans who have spearheaded many of the great conservation moments in our history: Nixon created the Environmental Protection Agency and signed the Clean Air Act, and George H.W. Bush signed a bill to curtail acid rain - one of the great environmental protection success stories. Ronald Reagan (1982) said *""If we've learned any lessons during the past few decades, perhaps the most important is that preservation of our environment is not a partisan challenge; it's common sense. Our physical health, our social happiness, and our economic well-being will be sustained only by all of us working in partnership as thoughtful, effective stewards of our natural resources."*. As with many issues that become political bargaining chips, it seems as if politicians and news agencies have decided on the parties' opinions and reinforce these to ensure loyalty in voters or readers, rather than delivering sincere, effective, and important policies or news.

## A personal journey across the left-right divide

I recall the agitation my partner, Michael, was displaying as we flew into Omaha for the first time for me to meet his family. He was making a long list of topics not to discuss and no doubt quietly hoping I wouldn't spew profanities, which was my western Massachusetts habit at that time. It was thus that the warning from Gandalf to Pippin, in the film *The Two Towers*, became a family joke: "Perhaps it's best if you don't speak at all". Here I was: this far-left environmental nonconformist astrophysicist from Amherst about to meet his extended clan of mid-western God-fearing conservatives. Some of them had never even met a vegetarian before. I had certainly never met an evangelical Christian before. And frankly, I assumed they were probably non-thinking sheep, who followed doctrine blindly, and adopted conservative policies primarily out of personal economic greed. Clearly, I was wrong. And I offer them my sincere apologies.

Over the years, my in-laws' kindness, commitment to their faith, and open-heartedness transformed my prejudice into respect and love. Indeed, my father-in-law is the wisest and most accepting man I've ever known. I love him dearly. My partner's brother and his wife invited my youngest son and me to live in their house in Nebraska, for a year, so our son could attend high school in the United States. You can't get much more open-minded and generous than that, especially when you consider how well they already knew me! My sister-in-law, Lori made me feel very welcome in their home creating a beautiful and peaceful haven for me in my adopted bedroom. And in addition to being lovely and brilliant, she is a homesteading wonder which is a key element for eco-living. My brother-in-law, Craig, was also very welcoming and helped me profoundly to write this book by talking with me about these issues in a succession of honest, intense, fun, and searching conversations. He really taught me that his world view is self-consistent and well thought out. Thank you, Craig and Lori.

My year in Nebraska was certainly one of personal growth. I lived as a minority, and sometimes it felt even more foreign than when our young family lived as the only Westerners in a small resort town in Japan. In particular, being in Omaha laid open my own lack of grace when dealing with people who don't share my liberal tendencies. For instance, I was paralyzed when my request to join a local gardening group was responded to with an e-mail that ended with the phrase "Gardening for Jesus". Fair enough, it was a church gardening group, but I didn't know if I should acknowledge my complex non-traditional-Christian worldview right off the bat, or keep it to myself, which felt duplicitous. In the end, I was so conflicted that I couldn't go. This well-meaning comment had inadvertently alienated me. How often had I done this to conservatives? All too often, I'm afraid.

My year in Omaha gifted me with a new appreciation that the tone of environmental conversations is probably alienating a lot of would-be environmentalist allies. Undoubtedly some conservatives are conservationists just as some liberals aren't. But I found that during my year in Omaha, the environment was rarely talked about. There were rarely any decent vegetarian options at restaurants, no green energy companies to choose from, and very little in the way of environmental activism, to name just a few examples. My environmental rants were sometimes of no interest to the people I met, shocking I know, and at other times probably were downright offensive. I therefore decided to write this book to try to explain, in a respectful and well-documented manner, the status of our natural world, why it is so worrying, and how easy it is to fix it.

As isolating as my time in Omaha felt with regard to the greater community, I had brilliant conversations with my relatives and my new friend, Diane, about environmental, social, and spiritual issues. What we found, and many of you probably already know, is that with the deepening of our mutual understanding, we uncovered far more in common than that which divided us. We all want our family and friends to be safe and secure, happy and well provided for. We all want to have meaningful work and relationships. We all want to live in nice communities with lots of green spaces. We all want social justice and peace. Of course, we sometimes differ in how we would go about achieving such goals. But especially at this point in our nation's history, we could do with more focus on what we do have in common. And if our common ground includes 'Nature is worth protecting', we can turn our society into one which nurtures the natural world.

## World out of balance: crisis and opportunity

We have more know-how and capability than ever before, so why does it feel as if we are busier than ever and blindly rushing toward disaster? Any way you slice it, it feels as if our systems are muddled and corrupted, and some of the results are shockingly unequal distributions of social, political, natural and personal wellbeing, and security.

It can be difficult to act on these issues, they can feel insurmountable, too numerous, or not our individual fault or responsibility. Or maybe we are already overwhelmed by life's chaos and don't want more chores or guilt. While I too feel many of these barriers to action, I also feel it is not only our responsibility to address these issues, but also that it isn't all that complicated to make the world a vastly better place with relatively simple and straightforward changes in our habits.

I'm unsure about a lot of things. I'm unsure about where my sons will be living in five years, about what I'll do after I've finished this book, or even what I'll have for lunch. But I am not unsure about what needs to be done to solve our environmental problems. After 35 years of environmental activism and 25 years of these also spent doing environmental scientific research, I'm convinced that the lynch-pin driver of most modern ills is money. It is through our spending patterns that economic, political, social, and lifestyle signals propagate and strengthen the patterns of modern society. Much of this is for good – we buy food and live in nice shelters, we give to charities. But much of our consumption is excessive. For example, each American is responsible for the extraction from the earth of 150 pounds of raw materials, EVERY SINGLE DAY, to support our life-styles. One hundred and fifty pounds of raw materials.

In North America, this 150 pound daily consumption habit is roughly evenly divided between extracting fossil fuels, biomass, and nonmetallic minerals (like gravel and sand), with metal ores

Environmental issues are not
specialist,
leftist, nor
insignificant.

Environmental issues are
urgent,
life threatening,
pervasive,
solvable, and
everyone's responsibility.

Reasons to protect nature:
survival,
moral responsibility,
security,
wealth equality,
intergenerational justice,
protect human health,
ensure future options,
protect fresh air,
ensure clean water,
protect healthy soil,
inherent value of wildlife,
protect biodiversity,
protect natural wealth,
spiritual value, and
recreational use.

accounting for the last 15%.[6] These materials are used to make the products we buy and power the services we access. I believe that many purchases of low-use or luxury items may not bring enough usefulness or joy to justify their resource use. And by too much resource use, I mean not only natural resources but also the time and money you have had to spend to acquire an item or service. Many people go further and state that we are actually stressed by this excess of stuff. For instance, Marie Kondo's advice to 'Get rid of anything which doesn't bring you joy' is hugely popular and is being applied across many sectors.

Critically, we have absolute control over how we spend our money. And while there's undoubtedly a hill to climb to achieve sustainable and just purchasing patterns, life on the other side of that hill is not only better for global, national, and local natural systems, it is potentially far better for us as well – with less stress, greater social wealth, more security, healthier lifestyles, and more time for love.

One important step to reducing our material consumption is a subtle yet powerful switch in our perception as to what gives us security. Somehow, modern life in the United States and the United Kingdom, the two places I've lived in recently, seems to be about the pursuit of security through amassing economic wealth. This is a false economy in the grossest sense. Our focus on financial well-being comes at great expense and threatens our very existence. We seem to have forgotten to pay attention to other forms of wealth such as natural capital, social wealth, and our health. I'll talk more about all of this in the coming chapters, but for now, just note that our monetary prioritization is such an entrenched and diseased part of our culture that it has been given the name 'Affluenza'[7] - a concatenation of affluence and influenza.

Chapters 2 and 3 explore how our consumption patterns are, without a doubt, driving the widespread devastation of the natural world. Not just for panda bears and tigers but for every ecosystem: the numbers of wild animals have declined dramatically, plastic is in every part of the ocean, soils are

---

[6] UNEP International Resource Panel 2016, "Global Material Flows and Resource Productivity"

[7] https://en.wikipedia.org/wiki/Affluenza accessed November 13, 2019

degrading, forests are disappearing, coral reefs are dying, and on and on. It seems so unfair to the other *8 million* species[8] with whom we 'share' this planet. Or for our grandchildren for that matter, how will future generations fare without forests? Will they have to eat laboratory-grown food and breathe artificially cleaned air and water?

Our drive for more stuff, at the lowest possible prices, has also driven the rise of shocking wealth disparity. Fifteen companies have revenue streams greater than three quarters of the *countries* in the world including Walmart, Apple, Amazon, Toyota, and CVS.[9, 10] This is echoed in the rising wealth disparity of individuals: eight men own more than 50% of the global population, and the richest 1% own more than the other 99% of us[11] - this cannot be fair or stable. Mingled in with these large-scale problems, Americans work more hours than ever before, leaving less time for family and fun, we are more depressed and lonely, we trust our neighbors less, and are in greater debt than ever before.[12] I'll discuss these social ills in detail in Chapter 5.

The fact that it is *consumers* who are ultimately driving the destruction of the natural world is the great elephant in the room. No product producer, no political party, no newspaper nor even an environmental charity wants to convey such a negative message. It would be bad for business. However, it is only through accepting the bitterness of this realization that can we reach the sweet center: *We can change the paradigm.* On a dime. The power to

---

[8] Mora, C. et al 2011, "How many species are there on earth and in the ocean?", PLoS Biol 9: e1001127 https://doi.org/10.1371/journal.pbio.1001127

[9] Forbes 2019 Ranking of World's Largest Public Companies https://www.forbes.com/global2000/list/2/#header:revenue_sortreverse:true accessed October 10, 2019

[10] Wikipidea "List of Countries by Government Budget" https://en.wikipedia.org/wiki/List_of_countries_by_government_budget accessed October 10, 2019

[11] Oxfam 2017, "An economy for the 99%", https://www.oxfamamerica.org/explore/research-publications/an-economy-for-the-99-percent/

[12] Schor , J. B. 2010 True Wealth, Penguin Books, New York and references therein

do so and to determine our future is in our hands, not in the power of our governments or multinational corporations. Politicians follow where the populace wants to go, as it should be. Corporations are only doing what they were set up to do – make money for their shareholders – but they can only continue to do this with our financial support. It is we, the populace, who have the freedom – and the responsibility inherent with that freedom – to choose politicians and corporations we support with our voting, purchasing, and our investment choices. It's pretty straightforward really.

## The ABCs of changing habits: belief, education and exposure

In the following chapters, I will set out the reasons why we must change our consumption patterns. While alarming, this is not alarmist. When you acknowledge what the many sources of data across a broad spectrum of resources are telling us, you'll realize that we are like locusts eating up our natural resources at an ever-accelerating pace. To survive, we need to change our habits from prioritizing financial and time costs to prioritizing well-being: ours and nature's. In theory, this is relatively simple: buy less stuff and invest wisely. Repair, share, make, and borrow stuff, and when we must buy, buy used and buy for the long-term. As for investments, we need to be confident that the money we spend on bills and services, for example on our mortgage, electric bill, or transportation, are supporting ethical companies. In practice, however, in addition to know-how and infrastructure, we must have the conviction that it's both important and urgent to change our consumption patterns, otherwise other cares will overshadow these concerns. With a steadfast conviction that we must overcome these problems we will find ways. It is our less-than-strong-conviction of the importance of living in more eco-conscious ways that remains the sticking point. This book will help to strengthen your conviction to live in a more eco-conscious way.

There are three key steps to changing behavior patterns: belief, education, and exposure. As our beliefs, education, and exposure change, we modify our behaviors. However, the path isn't always linear or straightforward. A personal example are my eating patterns. I gave up eating mammals more than 30 years ago because it made me sad to think of animals being treated poorly. And while I always wanted to be fully vegetarian, I never quite made that commitment because it was easier to eat chicken and fish when my family did. However, exposure to the issues during the research for this book, strengthened my belief to the point that I've transitioned to a much stricter vegetarian diet. And I'm very grateful for that. It's not that I hadn't read and thought about many of the environmental impacts of meat before, but somehow, at this point in my life, the stories sunk in deeper. We follow different paths in endeavoring to live up to our ideals, but belief, education, and exposure certainly play important parts in that journey.

## Belief

Belief that eco-action is a moral imperative, can be the key sticking point. In order for us to find some common ground here, it's helpful to consider two kinds of beliefs: fundamental convictions and derived beliefs. A fundamental conviction is not necessarily provable, but is rather felt to be self-evident or is an expression of faith, such as 'Nature has inherent value'. When we encounter someone who holds a different belief from us, remembering the distinction between belief which is based on faith and one that is derived from other precepts can be helpful. Sometimes we must accept that someone holds a different fundamental belief than we do, but we may still be able to find common derived beliefs and goals. At other times, we may find that a difference of opinion arises from different reasoning from the same fundamental belief. Whatever our differences, however, I have found that we can almost always find common ground. For instance, everyone I've ever spoken to about it believes 'We should preserve the natural world'. And this is a monumentally positive place to start.

But we can arrive at this conclusion, about the preservation of nature, in different ways. For instance, I think that nature has an inherent value. Not that it is more important than humans or to be worshipped, but because life is wonderful, awe-inspiring, beautiful, and unfathomable in many ways. Who am I to harm other life simply for my convenience? Other people may hold that nature has an inherent spiritual value, because it brings people closer to God. Many people, many Christians included, believe that 'Nature is worth saving' because protecting the environment is one of the most effective ways to care for the poor[13], as I outlined above. Or, we may believe that nature is God's creation and therefore we should respect it. And finally, we may be convinced of the imperative to protect nature because there are over 100 Bible verses that advocate caring for the environment.[14] Indeed, many Christians do work within their faith to protect nature.[15,16] Non-religious beliefs in the importance of nature also abound such as other beings' right to life, social justice, intergenerational justice, catastrophe avoidance, and preserving medicinal opportunities and genetic diversity.

## Education and trusted evidence

Knowing that the environment is under threat is, of course, fundamental to taking steps to protect it. And, once we've concluded that we should protect nature, we need to know how to do so. I presume it is an uncontroversial claim to state that education underpins effective responses to threats. But *how* we are educated is not without controversy. Our knowledge base arises from a broad array of actors: our families and community, our school, our news sources, our friends, and our own research. And while we may be exposed to many ideas and facts, those we accept are largely based on which sources we trust. Trust underlifes belief.

---

[13] Hayhoe, C. E. October 19, 2019, "I'm a climate scientist who believes in God. Hear me out", New York Times https://www.nytimes.com/2019/10/31/opinion/sunday/climate-change-evangelical-christian.html accessed November 13, 2019

[14] https://www.openbible.info/topics/caring_for_the_environment accessed November 14, 2019

[15] Caring for Creation https://www.elca.org/Faith/Faith-and-Society/Social-Statements/Caring-for-Creation

[16] https://www.learnreligions.com/christian-environmental-organizations-4590157 accessed November 15, 2019

Trust is an important ingredient for a happy society and one of the aspects of American culture which is most laudable. Americans collect and post mail in boxes that anyone could access, they assume cashiers will give them the correct change and tend to tell them if they notice they've been given too much. Americans ask for and give help to one another quite freely. But this trust is decaying. Research shows that we trust one another less and we socialize less than even a few decades ago[17]. Republicans trust Democrats less, and vice versa. And this is crippling.

Without trust in one another, it becomes impossible to solve problems. I'm not talking about blind trust, but rather open-eyed trust where, perhaps, we give people the benefit of the doubt. It would be productive if we could grant other people the grace of assuming they are decent human beings who are not trying to manipulate us, to believe that others have their own wisdom from which we can learn. It is my opinion that we have lost this gift in large part because large scale social forces benefit from us being divided and because some recent social trends reinforce our divisions.

In the past, we socialized with folks from our neighborhoods and families. But today, our families are more dispersed and we tend to socialize with people with whom we work or worship or with whom we share interests[18]. In the past, when we socialized with people in our neighborhoods or our families, we were thrown into relationships with people with different viewpoints than our own. We were reminded regularly that even though we may have a difference of opinions with family or friends, we could still respect and rely on others. But with interest-focused socialization growing, we are being exposed less and less to other ways of thinking.

The internet contributes to this like-to-like socialization. We tend to access articles, news, and discussion groups that back-up our viewpoints. Google even tailors our search results based on previous browsing history. For example, I'm unlikely to come

---

[17] Schor , J. B. 2010 True Wealth, Penguin Books, New York

[18] Putnam, R.D. 2000, Bowling alone: The collape and revival of American community, New York: Simon and Schuster

across articles on negative financial implications of environmental protection when I type in *impacts of rainforest conservation* into Google because my previous searches tend to be about environmental issues and not financial ones. I might not click on the ones that don't fit into my world view or interests anyway. And it has been shown time and again, that our political views are most strongly influenced not by education nor evidence, but by what our community thinks. As the mix of people in our social gatherings has shrunk, so too has our breadth of acceptance.

In addition to the influence our communities have on us, there are also two psychological reactions which act to further strengthen the walls around our world views – confirmation bias and the boomerang effect. Confirmation bias is the phenomenon whereby we seek out and recall facts which support our world view. We go even farther in that we *interpre*t stories in ways which strengthen our world view. So we can hear the same news story but come out with strengthened opinions that are diametrically opposed.

But our brains are even more devious than that at preserving our world view. It's been shown that facts which contradict our model of the world, also strengthen our world view. For a one-off ill-fitting data bomb, this may well be reasonable. I'm not likely to be convinced you just saw an English nanny floating in on an umbrella no matter how convinced you are. I will argue you were drunk, that it's physically impossible, or I'll simply refuse to believe you. But we take it further than just rejecting a piece of ill-fitting evidence. When presented with evidence contrary to our opinions, we aggressively seek out reasons to reject it – we look for counter studies, we doubt the source, we dig in our heels. We are often left feeling even stronger about our original thoughts. Together with confirmation bias, this boomerang effect strengthens our social groups. We believe even more that Trump or Obama is bad whenever we hear ANYTHING about them.

But even with greater like-for-like socialization and the foibles of the human psyche, I don't think we would be so divided if it weren't for big social organizations that seek to stir up our divisions. It seems to me as if politicians, many news sources, and corporations seem to have perfected the art of dividing society into groups so that they can put a fence around us and claim our loyalty in the shape of votes, readership, or money. They do this by misdirection, by muddying the waters, by focusing on emotional issues, or by pointing out the failings in "others". Our emotional response, which the politicians, news sources, and corporations well know, is far more powerful than our rational response and we are likely to fear and distrust the "other side" far more strongly. We are firmly bounced back into "our camp". This frothing up of the differences between us is used to serve the actor's ends, loyalty and financial gain, rather than to serve societal gains such as improved policies and programs or balanced news reporting. It is a pox.

In the past few decades, we have seen greater and greater political and social polarities. This polarity and focus on differences rather than shared common beliefs causes all kinds of social stress. It also muddies our thinking on how to respond to global crises: be it the refugee crisis, hunger, wars, financial inequity, or global warming. Rather than focusing on a common goal and working towards achieving it, we become stagnated arguing over derived beliefs such as "There should be greater gun control" versus "We should arm teachers" when we all agree there are too many gun-related deaths. Certainly, there must be solutions which should have been carried out decades ago.

Let me tell you about an experiment my brother-in-law and I carried out in which I caught myself exhibiting confirmation bias and the boomerang effect, in the midst of an attempt by a news agency to divide society along party lines. Craig and I decided to read one another's newspapers for a week, The Guardian for Fox News and vice versa. I literally couldn't remember the details of the anti-Hillary Clinton stories (confirmation bias), and, quite possibly was more sympathetic to her (boomerang effect). Not that I'm a fan of hers, but because I didn't trust Fox News to be unbiased towards her, that information just flowed right out of my brain. On the other hand, I did notice, and clearly remember, that Fox News took a phrase out of context from an Obama statement. A Fox headline read: "Obama rips Fox News viewers 'You are living on another planet' ". If that's what he said, that's pretty insulting but the full quote from Obama was: "If you watch Fox News, you are living on a different planet than you are if you are listening to NPR". "Fox News is untruthful and biased", I pranced around happily thinking. Upon reflection, however, my happy dance held a mirror up to my own biases, too, for I later figured out that the full quote was further down in the Fox News story. But, even though Fox News weren't telling an explicit lie, we must admit the Fox headline was hugely misleading and arguably immoral, for it implies Obama was insulting Fox viewers rather than saying their world view is different from those who listen to NPR. I think we can all agree that that is true.[19]

As part of our growing lack of trust, there is now a trend to dismiss research with which we don't agree. A friend told me that if I start a sentence with "A study shows..." that it actually deterred from his belief in the subsequent statement. A UK politician, Michael Gove, recently said "We have had enough of experts" and just last week I heard someone on the radio use the phrase "self-appointed experts". To me, these are Orwellian and disturbing twists of modern society. It's not consistent either, for we trust doctors, air traffic controllers, architects, and so forth. We seek out expert advice when we have complex taxes to file, a leaky roof, or a computer problem to solve. We are now witnessing a tidal wave of dismissal, facilitating the draining of the very life out of us.

## Exposure

Beyond trusting evidence and the conviction that eco-action is a moral imperative, a further element influencing our adoption of eco-behavior is exposure to the impacts of resource hungry behaviors. Meeting with folks who are pondering the same kinds of questions helps, as do reading, talking, and listening to podcasts about the issues. Without this kind of nourishment, our convictions can falter. By talking with or learning about the opinions of people different from yourself, you are expanding and softening your bubble. You are battling the trust deficit, taking back control of your own opinions.

Perhaps this book will challenge you in the same way as living in Nebraska challenged me. Many of the things I feel most

---

[19] https://www.foxnews.com/entertainment/obama-rips-fox-news-viewers-you-are-living-on-a-different-planet accessed November 13.2019

strongly about were challenged by society there: what food I ate, my obsession with saving the environment, how I raised my kids. It sure made me more understanding and sympathetic to the conservative worldview. In return, I hope this book helps some people understand that making eco-conscious choices can arise from a consistent worldview grounded on honorable beliefs. If reading this is exposing you to a different worldview, good on you for making the world a better place in a way that may not be easy or comfortable but is truly bubble breaking. Pop, pop, pop.

## Some thoughts on being a climate scientist

For my PhD in astrophysicist, I ran computer models of star formation and intergalactic gas flows. During a post-doctoral fellowship, doing exciting research into whether or not shock waves could trigger star formation, I grew increasingly compelled to use my career to help save the environment for others – other people, other generations, and other species. As the star formation models have at their core the same physics of sloshing gases into and out of imaginary boxes as do climate models, I delved into modeling climate change impacts on ecosystems.

The first ecological study I was involved in gained broad international recognition and press coverage when we showed that it was plausible that climate change had driven the extinctions of 70 species of frogs from the anuran order, which decades before had numbered 110 species.[20] These are brightly colored frogs who breed in rivers making it fairly easy to find them and document their extinctions. It was both the most exciting work and the most depressing work I'd ever done - it was also one of the first attempts to document that modern climate change was driving extinctions. As is often the case, the story was more complicated than we originally postulated, and it is now generally believed that the direct cause of death of the frogs is a fungus, which may have gained traction because of ongoing shifts in the local cloudiness regime. After that initial study, I continued working on how climate dictates what kind of ecosystem thrives where and also exploring

[20] Pounds, J.A. et al 2006, "Widespread amphibian extinctions from epidemic disease driven by global warming", Nature 439, 161

carbon and other gas exchanges between the atmosphere and the ground. The land surface is important for the global carbon cycle because the land absorbs around 30% of the greenhouse gases we emit.[21] There are worries this will change in the coming decades to soil becoming a *source* of carbon dioxide rather than its current status of being a *sink* of carbon dioxide.[22] This is one of the positive feedbacks which climate scientists warn may mean we only have until 2030 to really get our act together and drastically reduce emissions.[23]

All told, I spent 30 years in academia, 10 as an astrophysicist and 20 as a climate-ecosystem physicist. I didn't like being an academic, and supported by my partner I've recently quit to pursue gardening and sustainable living and to write this book. I was competent and clever enough, I like to believe, and there was ample opportunity for me in academia, but I was never as focused as most academics. The reason I'm telling you about my experiences is manifold. First of all, I am a climate and ecosystem expert and, hopefully, this means you will trust that I know the subject matter of this book. But also, to assure you that I do not have a personal agenda in writing this book. I am not out to gain your money, make a name for myself, or to gather popularity. My only agenda is to protect nature and reduce the perceived divide between environmentalists and others.

But by laying open some of my experiences in climate change science, I also hope to illuminate the fact that climate science, in particular, is not a fraternity of conspiring geeks set out to mislead the public and get money from governments. My experience taught me that the world of climate science is a brutal,

---

[21] IPCC, 2014: *Climate Change 2014: Synthesis Report. Contribution of Working Groups I, II and III to the Fifth Assessment Report of the Intergovernmental Panel on Climate Change* [Core Writing Team, R.K. Pachauri and L.A. Meyer (eds.)]. IPCC, Geneva, Switzerland, 151 pp.

[22] Green, J.K. et al 2019, "Large influence of soil moisture on long term terrestrial carbon uptake", Nature 565, 476-479.

[23] IPCC 2015, *Global Warming of 1.5°C. An IPCC Special Report on the impacts of global warming of 1.5°C above pre-industrial levels and related global greenhouse gas emission pathways, in the context of strengthening the global response to the threat of climate change, sustainable development, and efforts to eradicate poverty.*

competitive, and intense arena for delving into what is going on with our planet's atmosphere today. Competition is fierce, there is occasional backbiting and an utterly rigorous review system for publications. This was very unlike the gentle world of astronomy from which I came. I published one climate paper which required 10 resubmissions even though the work remained fundamentally as it was at the start, but it challenged a commonly used method. With perseverance, the scientific process led to the work being published. Albeit, it contributed to my being worn down by the competitiveness of the field and my general discontent at living in books all the time. However, as disillusioned as I am about the worth of spending my own life in academia, I am not disillusioned about the scientific process. At no time, never, did I encounter falsification of data, misrepresentation of results, or anything other than a pursuit of understanding nature. And if you've ever known a scientist, you will know very well that scientists like to argue. With pretty much anything you have to say. The idea that scientists as a community would agree on a conspiracy to "sell" to the public is beyond far-fetched. If data and theories were being presented which were based on falsehoods, there is not a single group of people who would like to prove others wrong more than scientists. It is only truth that can withstand the onslaught of a rigorous and dogged army of academics.

Fundamental to this book being effective is for you to trust that I am doing my best to present facts. I have done loads of background research for this book and aim to present only well-documented conclusions. I provide references for the data I present and I've tried to get most of these from large-scale reviews provided by the United Nations (UN), the World Health Organization (WHO), or similar organizations. I used reports for which a broad group of experts have reviewed tens or even hundreds of other studies in the literature and summarized the state of our knowledge on these issues. So the reports I'm referencing are not like the flip-flopping headlines we're all familiar with such as: "Eggs are bad for you" to "Eggs are superfoods" back to "Eggs will kill you" headlines. Those types of headlines can arise from single studies that might, for instance, only consider the implications of eggs for a single organ rather than the whole body.

In addition to my academic career, I've also been engaged in environmental activism most of my life. My activities have included helping write a sustainability charter for a city, organizing round table discussions between city planners, citizens, business people, and non-governmental organizations (NGOs), starting an e-mail discussion group which morphed into ECOJAM, and working on the Great Ape Project. I've also been active in community efforts such as early days recycling, community gardening, carrying out enrichment activities at zoos, and picking up litter.

In conclusion, allow me to reiterate that the battle to save the natural world is not one of left versus right, nor of conservative versus liberal, and not even of concerned citizens versus corporations. It is not an "us" versus "them" problem, but rather a series of crises in which we all must acknowledge our part, and then change our destructive behavior. And the beauty of it is that the change is not onerous or punitive, but rather opportunistic and joyful. Addressing environmental issues enables us to reconnect to those things we know are important but which we've become adept at smoothing over. It's like we are playing a game of chicken, racing towards a cliff edge in a hot rod, and worse yet, we've got a blindfold on. Peaking out of the blindfold we see all kinds of warning signs and rough territory so we choose to keep the blindfold on. But if we don't change our direction *we are* going over the cliff. The irony is that if we simply take off the blindfold, we'll see there is a green field full of wildflowers, songbirds, and dear friends to which we can readily divert our course if we'd grit our teeth, turn the wheel, and ride out a few bumps. We know it is the right thing to do. This alternative reality has always been here. Let's work to get there – together.

# 2 THE STATE OF THE 8

## STATUS OF EIGHT ESSENTIAL NATURAL RESOURCES

There is a dizzying array of environmental crises presented to us in the media. During the month leading up to writing these lines, there have been the following news stories: 1. 60% of wild vertebrates have disappeared since 1970[24], 2. 90% of the world's children breathe polluted air[25], 3. coral reefs are likely to be wiped from the planet in 50 years[26] and 4. the UN has warned that if we don't halt the destruction of the environment we may well face our own extinction[27].

We have evidence from satellite imagery of shrinking glaciers, a poleward creep of the treeline, high rates of deforestation, and large scale conversion of wild grasslands to managed agriculture. If we dig deeper, there are issues of toxic pollutants in soils, rivers, and the very air we breathe, causing developmental disruption in children, as well as disease and death in adults. Nature is showing signs of stress. These include widespread and numerous extinctions, increasingly earlier bud burst and later leaf fall, stressed fisheries, and frightfully low bee and other insect numbers. And more recently, it is likely that the

---

[24] WWF. 2018. Living Planet Report 2018. Aiming Higher. Grooten, M. and Almond, R.E.A.(Eds). WWF, Gland, Switzerland.

[25] https://www.theguardian.com/environment/2018/oct/29/air-pollution-worlds-children-breathing-toxic-air-who-study-finds

[26] https://www.theguardian.com/environment/2018/nov/11/next-generation-may-never-see-coral-reefs

[27] https://www.theguardian.com/environment/2018/nov/03/stop-biodiversity-loss-or-we-could-face-our-own-extinction-warns-un

Covid-19 pandemic is the direct result of closer contact with animals, with 70% of all emergent diseases originating in wildlife and domesticated animals. Indeed, as we destroy more nature and partake in intensive farming, we are exposing ourselves to an estimated 1.7 million viruses in animals of the kind known to infect people.[28]

It can be challenging to assess what all these reports mean for global environmental systems. Just because one species or location shows loss, does that mean that the system as a whole is stressed? Although we know bees are doing poorly, is it perhaps the case that all other insects are thriving? Is there a skew in what is reported - do we only hear about the worrying aspects and wildlife as a whole is healthy? In this chapter, I will give an overview of the system rather than focusing on specific reports.

As a physicist, I am trained to look at whole systems, and to search for and explain patterns in the natural world. And that's the approach I take in this book by considering the following two questions: 1. "What do our physical bodies need to survive and thrive?", and 2. "What is the status of these resources on a global scale?". The answer to the first question leads to the identification of 8 natural resources, which are essential for healthy human life: fresh air, clean water, and so forth. To understand the status of these resources, I present global measures, or indicators, of these resources. These indicators are derived and calculated in large scale studies that summarize and rely on the work of many previously published articles. In this way, we avoid the diversion that these issues may be local problems or unreliable results. I endeavor to present the status of these eight life-sustaining resources in a manner that will enable you to decide whether or not we need to change how we are using these resources.

A summary of the status of our 8 essential resources is presented in the *Planetary Wheel*, a figure created for this book to illustrate the global trends in how much of these resources we

---

[28] Settele, J. et al 2020, "COVID-19 stimulus measures must save lives, protect livelihoods and safeguard nature to reduce the risk of future pandemics", published online 27 April, 2020 by https://ipbes.net/covid19stimulus

have used. This figure shows, in most cases, the fraction of the resource remaining as measured by three different aspects for each resource. This figure is really the heart of this chapter.

If you take away nothing else from this chapter, aim to grasp the magnitude of the current level of depletion of earth's natural resources. If we simply average all measures given in the *Planetary Wheel* figure, we'd find that only 27% of Earth's resources remain. This, of course, is a rough and flawed approach, not least because it mixes in different kinds of measures. Some of the measures are resource use relative to safe operating spaces rather than physical spaces, like acres of forest. Nonetheless, the percentage, 27%, does serve to warn that we are in serious danger of depriving future generations of life.

My goal when I started this book was to identify, quantify, and rank effective practical actions one person could take to save the natural world and ourselves. I wanted to calculate numbers for the *magnitude* of the impact of our various activities, such as meat production or operating a computer, on the 8 resources. Then we could have readily figured out what changes would have the largest positive impact on the environment. I laugh now as I recall that because that plan was insanely naive. I did, however, find an answer, just not to the question I initially posed. I found that there is one aspect of our lives which accounts for 20-80% of the ongoing depletion of most of our eight natural resources - and that is our food production. If we consider transport and running our homes, together with food production, these three activities account for the vast majority of the loss of all of our natural resources. But I get ahead of myself. Let's get started with that discussion of the natural resources we need to survive.

## What are the essential natural resources which sustain life?

If we think about what a human needs to survive over increasing time periods, from seconds to days to centuries, we can readily list what humanity needs to survive. And all of these needs are met by natural systems. Through out this book, I use the term "resource" to refer to these essential life sustaining chunks of nature. However, the term "resource" may encourage some to think that these chunks-of-nature are for-humanity's-exclusive-use and free-for-the-taking. But the natural world is neither of these. The removal of ecosystems always results in a greater cost than what was gained by its removal and there are millions other species, not to mention future humans, who rely on intact ecosystems. It is with a heavy dose of reluctance that I use the term resource, but do so as a convenient shorthand and to remind us that these natural resources are essential for humanity's very survival.

To survive beyond a few minutes, we need fresh air, and to survive beyond a few days, we need fresh water. Therefore, we'll consider clean water and air as our first two essential life-sustaining natural resources. When we shift up to weekly timescales, we need food. To produce food, we need viable soils, predictable weather, freshwater, and pollinators. Thus we add healthy soils and a stable climate as are our 3rd and 4th natural resources. Pollinators need healthy natural ecosystems, making wilderness our 5th key natural resource. A robust wilderness is the cornerstone for all life, for as well as supporting all food production, it also cleans the water we drink and the air we breathe.

When we increase our timescale to decades, we recognize that diversity of plants, animals and fungi are essential for adaptation making diversity of life, or biodiversity, our 6th essential natural resource. The adaptability of life is essential for survival even in the absence of humanity's impacts. However, it is even more critical in the face of the stresses which our activities inflict upon the web of life, including habitat destruction, declining populations, invasive species, new diseases, and shifting weather patterns. Biological diversity allows some individuals to survive new situations and stresses, even if the bulk of the population is destroyed.

The added resiliency arising from diversity is true across spatial scales: from genetic diversity to species' diversity and all the way up to ecosystem diversity. Importantly for humans, diversity in our crops, pollinators and soil are the foundation of resilient agriculture. This is important for producing nutritious foods today, as well as for developing strains of crops which can deal with the conditions tomorrow which will include changing pest, disease, competition, and climate stresses. Biodiversity is a priceless resource essential for food security. On human lifespan timescales, biodiversity and wilderness also underpin health and well-being. For example, at least 50% of all medicines in clinical use today are derived from plants.[29, 30]

The 7th essential natural resource, healthy oceans, provides services to humans across all these timescales, from seconds to millenia. The oceans produce over half the oxygen we breathe, provide much of our food and medicine, and transport heat to high latitudes, making them far more habitable. Economically, 76% of all U.S. trade relies on marine transport. In the U.S. alone, ocean businesses employ 3,000,000 people and produce $282 billion of goods and services every year.[31]

And finally, while the above 7 resources are actual things we wish to protect, the last essential resource, involves something we want to prevent - toxic pollution. Including a toxicant free environment as the 8th natural resource, highlights the fact that we could conceivably have an abundance of other resources but no human life or severely degraded quality of life. Included in a toxicant-free environment are things like no lead poisoning, no mercury in our fish, no asbestos in our lungs, no plastics degrading into our food chain. You get the idea.

As a useful summary, consider that good health of humans directly requires six of our eight key resources: freshwater, clean air, wilderness, biodiversity, healthy soil, and a toxicant free environment. If we expand to longer timescales, good health also requires a stable climate and healthy oceans.

Could we have a different set of life-sustaining resources? Undoubtedly. But these eight make a good framework for

---

[29] Gurib-Fakim A. Medicinal plants: traditions of yesterday and drugs of tomorrow. Mol Aspects Med. 2006 Feb;27(1):1-93. Epub 2005 Aug 18. Review. PubMed PMID: 16105678.

[30] Incidentally, this makes it inaccurate to consider herbal medicine "alternative" or worse yet to dismiss it. The practice of claiming proven herbal medicines as part of "modern medicine" and dismissing unproven ones as alternative medicine is an unfair unsorting mechanism.

[31] https://oceanservice.noaa.gov/facts/why-care-about-ocean.html accessed December 29, 2019

considering what needs to be protected for humanity to thrive. They also mesh well with the hundreds of reports and articles I've read and the conversations I've had over my career on the state of our natural resources. Assuringly, this list of 8 resources is nearly the same as a list which a group of researchers from the Stockholm Resilience Centre used in their highly cited paper on planetary boundaries. Planetary boundaries are regularly used by local, national, and international policy makers and are discussed more below.

## Estimating resource status

In the rest of this chapter, I discuss the current state of these eight life-sustaining resources. There are several ways to go about estimating their status.

### *Estimating Resource Status: Fractions Remaining.*

Perhaps the most straightforward way to measure the condition of our natural resources is to assess what remains of a given resource, for instance, 68% of global forests remain[32]. I show this statistic as a slice of pie in *the Planetary Wheel* figure in the Wild Lands category with 68% of the slice in the black and white map of the earth and the lost 32% greyed out. The more black and white on the figure, the more of the resource that remains. Because a lot of the data is human-centric, I also include figures for how many people still have adequate access to a resource. For instance, only 29% of irrigated farms are estimated to have ample water, so this is shown as 29% of a slice of pie remaining in the freshwater category.[33]

### *Estimating Resource Status: Safe Operating Limits.*

A second way of assessing a resource's status is to determine what fraction of the resource we use, relative to what is 'safe' or sustainable for us to use. Researchers at the Stockholm

---

[32] Adams, E.E. 2012, "World Forest Area Still on the Decline", Earth Policy Institute

[33] Mekonnen, M.M. and A. Y. Hoekstra 2016, "Four billion people facing severe water scarcity", Sci. Adv., e1500323

Resilience Centre have calculated these safe use limits by identifying what fraction of a natural resource we have already used relative to safe consumption levels. The safe use limit is estimated based on the rate at which the given resource is regenerated. The researchers call these safe consumption levels 'planetary boundaries.' For example, for freshwater the key variable was identified as the *volume* of water withdrawals. The safe operating limit was defined as *how much water could be withdrawn* without creating regime change to aquatic ecosystems. Steffan and co-authors estimated that humanity withdraws 2600 cubic kilometers every year and that the planetary boundary level is 4000 cubic kilometers every year.[34] Thus we are using 59% of our safe water withdrawals. Therefore, *the Planetary Wheel* shows one of the slices in the freshwater category at 41%, the fraction of safe withdrawals remaining.

These estimates of our operating level relative to the safe planetary boundary are, of course, rough and rely somewhat on expert opinion. However, they are probably the best estimates on the state of a broad array of global natural resources using a common framework.

Similarly to the planetary boundary analysis, eco-footprints estimate how much land is required to support our lifestyles relative to how much is safe to use. In the eco-footprint case, '"the safe'" usage rate is based on how much land is needed to replenish the resource. Eco-footprints are a very popular and useful metric measuring how much land is required to support our lifestyles. They  are similar to the planetary boundary estimates in that they show how close we are to a maximum capacity. I discuss both the planetary boundary cases and the eco-footprint measure more in the text below.

## *Estimating Resource Status:  Miscellaneous.*

In addition to presenting fractions remaining and safe operating space estimates, there are a few pie slices in *the Planetary Wheel* for which I had to take a different approach.  For

[34] Steffen, W. et al, 2015, "Planetary boundaries: guiding human development on a changing planet", Science Express Jan 15, 2015, 10.1126/science.1259855

example, I wanted to acknowledge the large number of deaths attributed to polluted air, in the fresh air section. However, it is tricky to present that as a fraction. I discuss these "miscellaneous estimates" in the respective sections below.

In the remainder of this chapter, I discuss the status of these eight life-sustaining resources, in particular presenting their status in the figure the *Planetary Wheel*. But before we go into those details, I'd like to give my opinion on the fact that one of these resources underpins all of the others: wilderness. To have a flourishing wilderness, we need all the other resources to be robust. Furthermore, saving the wilderness may be seen as a self-evident extension of the ideology that we should love our neighbors, for the destruction of the wilderness hurts the world's poor the most. Many of us will also hold that wild things are also deserving of our love and respect. Finally, a focus on wilderness highlights the fact that every little bit we do is effective. Saving the wilderness does not have to be a 100% success or 100% failure outcome. Each time we choose to refill a water bottle rather than buy a plastic bottle makes a difference.

## I. Clean air

Roughly 1 in 8 premature deaths, globally, is linked to air pollution, that's around 7 million deaths a year. Outdoor air pollution ranks as the 6$^{th}$ leading contributor to premature death, while its companion, indoor air pollution, ranks 8$^{th}$. In the Planetary Resource Wheel figure, I've shown these premature deaths as a 0%, not knowing how else to represent 7 million premature deaths as a percentage. Also in the figure, I've shown the fraction of people who live in areas that meet the World Health Organization's (WHO) targets for clean air. Only 5% of us live in places which have air which passes WHO's Air Quality Guideline, which is 10 micrograms or less per cubic meter of particles 2.5 micrometers or smaller. WHO also set a series of interim targets, with the least stringent being to have less than 35 micrograms per

*Figure 2.1 PLANETARY WHEEL*
*Fraction Remaining of Global Life Sustaining Resources*

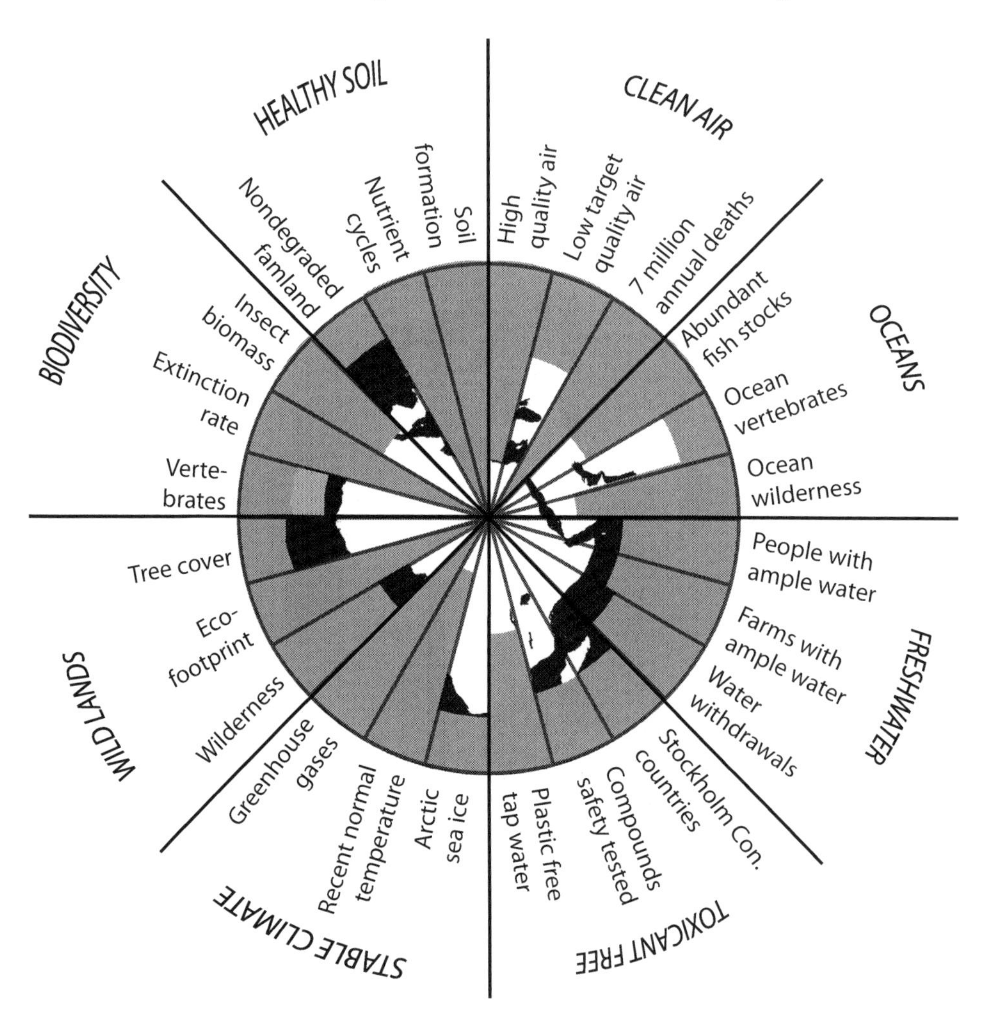

**Table 2.1 Notes on the Planetary Wheel Figure**

| | Measure | No. | Notes |
|---|---|---|---|
| Clean air | High quality air | 0.05 | People whose air quality meets WHO's recommended air quality guidelines (A) |
| | Low target quality air | 0.42 | People whose air quality meets WHO's least stringent air quality target. (A) |
| | * 7 million annual deaths | 0.0 | Indoor and outdoor air pollution lead to unacceptable number of deaths (B) |
| Oceans | Abundant fish stocks | 0.2 | Of documented world fish stocks, 80% are depleted, fully or over exploited (C) |
| | Vertebrates | 0.64 | Ocean vertebrates in 2012 vs 1971 (D) |
| | Ocean wilderness | 0.13 | Map of 15 human stressors finds 13% of the ocean has very little stress (E) |
| Freshwater | People with ample water | 0.29 | People without moderate to severe water scarcity at least one month per year (F) |
| | Farms with ample water | 0.29 | 71% of irrigated farms experience at least periodic water shortage (G) |
| | * Water withdrawals | 0.35 | Water withdrawals which will not severely degrade ecosystems (H) |
| Toxicant free | Stockholm Con. Countries | 0.51 | Parties to Stockholm Convention on Hazardous Waste meeting reporting targets (I) |
| | Compounds safety tested | 0.50 | Fraction of 5000 synthesized compounds with nearly universal human exposure (J) |
| | Plastic free tap water | 0.19 | Long, non-natural fibers found in most tap water, beer and salt (K) |
| Climate | Arctic Sea Ice | 0.61 | Sea ice in 2019 relative to 1981 (L) |
| | Recent normal Temp | 0.05 | 19 of the hottest 20 years, since 1884, have occurred since 2001 (L) |
| | * Greenhouse | 0.0 | Manmade heating 2.3x safe boundary(H) |
| Wildlands | Wilderness | 0.25 | Ice free land classified as wild (M) |
| | * Ecofootprint | 0.0 | Land use exceeds rate of renewal by factor of 1.7 (N) |
| | Tree cover | 0.68 | 68% of its historical value (O) |

| | | | |
|---|---|---|---|
| Biodiversity | Vertebrates | 0.42 | Of 14,000 populations of wild animals only 42% of animals remain vs 1971 (D) |
| | * Extinction rate | 0.0 | Extinction rate 100-1000 higher than safe boundary (H) |
| | Insect biomass | 0.24 | In 63 nature reserves, flying insect biomass at 76% of 1989 levels (P) |
| Healthy soil | Nondegraded farmland | 0.67 | Moderately to severely degraded by erosion, compaction, acidification & pollution (Q) |
| | * Nutrient cycles | 0.0 | Phosphorous is twice and nitrogen is 3 times the limit to avoid eutrophication (H) |
| | * Soil erosion vs formation | 0.0 | Conventional plowing soil erosion is 10 to 100 faster than soil replenishment (R) |

**No.** in the table heading is the fraction of a given measure of a resource remaining shown as the black and white Earth. Lost resources are colored grey. To represent the fraction remaining in the Planetary Wheel Figure, I show the fraction remaining as a proportion of area in a given wedge rather than showing the fraction remaining as the radius of the wedge. Thus, the figure does not exaggerate the amount of the resource that has been lost.

*: Measures noted with an asterix are not fractions of a remaining resource. Most of these cases represent the fraction of the resource relative to a safe operating space, as in the eco-footprint and the planetary boundary measures. Also, 7,000,000 premature deaths listed under Fresh Air are not a fraction, but are included to highlight the high rate of premature deaths.

References in Table 2.1

(A) Health Effects Inst. 2018. State of Global Air
(B) https://www.who.int/health-topics/air-pollution
(C) UNFAO 2008 State of World Fisheries & Aquaculture
(D) WWF International 2016, Living Planet Report
(E) Jones et al 2018, Current Biology 28, 1-7
(F) Mekomen & Hoekstra 2016 Science Advances
(G) Brauman et al 2016, Elementa 4:000083
(H) Steffan et al 2015, Science Jan 15, 2015
(I) UN The Sustainable Development Goals Report 2017
(J) The Lancet Commission on Pollution & Healthy, 2018, Lancet 391
(K) Kosuth 2018, PLoS One 13(4): e0194970
(L) NASA, climate.nasa.gov/vital-signs
(M) UNCCD Global Land Outlook 2017
(N) Lin et al 2018 Resources. 7(3): 58
(O) Adams 2012, Earth Policy Institute, World forest area still on the decline
(P) Hallman et al 2017 PLoS One 12:10
(Q) UNFAO & ITPS 2015 Status of the World's Soil Resources
(R) Montgomery, D. 2017, PNAS 104, p 13268

cubic meter, still 3.5 times the healthy level. Only 42% of the global population has air that meets this target.[35]

These numbers quite shocked me. But the mortality numbers are only the tip of the iceberg. Air pollution is associated with pneumonia, bronchitis, asthma, low birth weight, pre-term delivery, higher rates of early fetal loss, and is linked to disruptions in physical and cognitive development.[36] Sadly, urban air quality is getting worse,[37] and projections suggest that under 5 mortality will be 50% - 100% higher by 2050.[38] Indeed, WHO states that "air pollution is the single biggest environmental health threat."[39] Encouragingly, it is very cost-effective to clean up our air. A comprehensive review of air pollution found that for every dollar spent on reducing air pollution, there were $30 in benefits.[40]

## II. Oceans

Do we all have a deep longing for the oceans? I do. I want to be near them, be in them, be on them. I love their sparkling light, their rhythmic sounds, their moods, and the creatures that live in them. Dolphins, whales, manta rays, angelfish, starfish, coral reefs - all are profoundly beautiful. Oceans, of course, cover ⅔ of the earth's surface and range in depth from the inches and feet we interact with on the shore to six miles deep at the Mariana

---

[35] Health Effects Institute. 2018. State of Global Air 2018. Special Report. Boston, MA:Health Effects Institute. World Health Organization, '7 Million Premature Deaths Annually Linked to Air Pollution'

[36] WHO Review of evidence on health aspects of air pollution - REVIHAAP Project, 2011, Technical Report, downloaded from http://www.euro.who.int/ data/assets/pdf file/0004/193108/REVIHAAP-Final-technical-report-final-version.pdf?ua=1 on October 1, 2018

[37] American Lung Association, 'Air Pollution and Children's Health', 2003, accessed 13 July 2016.

[38] Rees, N. Et al 2016, "Clear the Air for Children: The impact of air pollution on children", UNICEF, ISBN: 978-92-806-4854-6

[39]https://www.theguardian.com/environment/2014/mar/25/air-pollution-single-biggest-environmental-health-risk-who

[40] Landrigan, P. et al 2017, "The Lancet commission on pollution and health", *Lancet* 2018, 319: 462:512

Trench. At that depth, the weight of water creates a pressure 1000 times that felt at the surface of the earth. One might think that this vastness would stop our having much impact on the oceans. But humans are many, and our consumption is vast. Disregard for the health of the oceans has led to the disturbingly long list of oceanic environmental problems. These include a 36% decrease in the number of vertebrates living in the ocean in 2002 relative to 1970[41] and 80% of fish stocks being either fully or overly exploited.[42] Both of which are shown on the *Planetary Wheel* figure.

In no particular order the crises unfolding in the ocean which I address below are dead zones, ocean acidification, loss of coral reefs, plastic garbage and microbeads in the ocean, and rising sea level and rising ocean temperature. I don't address the additional issues of pollution from tanneries, dye factories, sewage, pharmaceuticals, and vast numbers of other industries. Even if you don't live anywhere near an ocean, your choices about fish, meat, clothing, plastics, and carbon emissions have direct consequences on the seas.

*Dead zones and eutrophication.* The same process of eutrophication and oxygen depletion, which leads to unhealthy river ecosystems, can kill off ocean ecosystems near the coast. Recall that eutrophication arises when nutrient-rich runoff from livestock, over-fertilized fields, or sewage, drains into a body of water. The consequent nutrient dump causes an algal bloom in the water that consumes much or all of the available oxygen. Depleted oxygen levels lead to reductions in or complete elimination of the plants and animals at the base of the food chain, thus decreasing biodiversity and altering nutrient and other chemical cycles. Ocean areas with damagingly low oxygen levels have increased six-fold since 1970 and now cover several million square kilometers. Dead zones in the ocean have increased by a factor of 10 since 1950 to number 500 such sites. For example, the dead zone where the Mississippi drains into the Gulf of Mexico

---

[41] World Wildlife Fund. 2016. Living Planet Report 2016. Risk and resilience in a new era. WWF International, Gland, Switzerland

[42] Food and Agricultural Organization of the United Nations 2009, The State of the World's Fisheries and Aquaculture 2008,

reached a record size in 2017 of 8776 square miles, 50% larger than the historical average.[43]

*Acidification.* It is undisputed that the amount of carbon dioxide, $CO_2$, in the atmosphere has risen by 50% since before the pre-industrial revolution. While some people don't believe this has led to human-induced climate change, there is no disputing a human-driven rise of $CO_2$ in the atmosphere. This rise in atmospheric carbon impacts the carbon concentration in the oceans. In the absence of human emissions of carbon dioxide, the atmosphere-ocean carbon exchange was in balance and the concentration of carbon in the atmosphere and the ocean stayed relatively constant over time. But now that balance has shifted, rising levels of atmospheric $CO_2$ push more $CO_2$ into the ocean.

Carbon atoms from $CO_2$ react with water to eventually create hydrogen ions (H+), an acid. Due to the rise of oceanic $CO_2$, the concentration of H+ ions in the oceans has increased by almost 30% since pre-industrial times. This rise is called ocean acidification, and it is disrupting marine organisms' metabolic rates and immune systems. It is also implicated in coral bleaching and disruptions in the oceans' food chain. For this reason alone, and entirely independent from climate change issues, 105 science academies have recommended that we reduce our $CO_2$ emissions by 50% below 1990 levels by 2050.[44] The safe planetary boundary study identifies a safe level of acidity in the ocean as an essential natural limit to stay below. Disturbingly, we've already exceeded this safe boundary limit and therefore, the current level of ocean acidification is shown as 0% in one of the oceanic slices in the *Planetary Wheel* figure.[45]

*Coral reefs.* Sadly, we are in genuine danger of losing coral reefs all across the world. It is not only our enjoyment of these magnificent places which is threatened. Although coral reefs

---

[43] Breitburg, D. et al 2018, "Declining oxygen in the global ocean and coastal water" Science Vol. 359, Issue 6371, eaam7240 DOI: 10.1126/science.aam7240

[44] See Wikipedia page and references there https://en.wikipedia.org/wiki/Ocean_acidification, accessed November 4, 2018

[45] Steffen, W. et al, 2015, "Planetary boundaries: guiding human development on a changing planet", Science Express Jan 15, 2015, 10.1126/science.1259855

occupy a relatively small land area, 0.1% of the ocean floor, they are estimated to support between 1 and 8 million species, some 25% of the ocean's creatures.[46] Coral reefs are considerable contributors to human society by providing fertile fishing grounds, medicines, and protection of shorelines from large waves and storm surges. In total, it is estimated that reefs generate $375 billion in goods and services each year.[47] Coral reefs are impacted by a deadly cocktail of anthropogenic damage from ocean acidification, rising temperatures and sea levels, as well as pollution, tourism, and irresponsible fishing. In the late 2000s, it was determined that 27% of coral reefs were dead following a dramatic period of coral reef bleaching in 1998.[48] Around the same time, it was estimated that Caribbean shallow coral cover, a broad indicator of coral reef health, had shrunk from 50% in 1977 to just 10-15% in 2001.[49] More recently, McClenachan et al 2017 have used historical maps to show that we have already lost 52% of the coral reefs off the Florida keys.[50] Meanwhile, coral cover in the northern part of the Great Barrier Reef dropped from 50% to 10% in the two years between 2014 and 2016.[51] It is estimated

---

[46] UNEP Coral Reef Unit accessed October 28, 2018 http://coral.unep.ch/Coral_Reefs.html

[47] National Ocean Service branch of National Oceanic and Atmospheric Administration of the US Department of Commerce, "The Importance of Coral Reefs", downloads on October 23, 2018 from https://oceanservice.noaa.gov/education/tutorial_corals/coral07_importance.html

[48] Global Coral Reef Monitoring Network 2000, Status of the Coral Reefs of the World: 2000, edited by C. Wilkinson

[49] Millenium Ecosystem Assessment: Carribean Sea Ecosystem Assessment 2002, https://www.millenniumassessment.org/en/SGA.Carsea.html accessed July 12, 2019

[50] McClenachan, L. et al 2017, "Ghost reefs: Nautical charts document large spatial scale of coral reef loss over 240 years", Science Advances 3:e1603255

[51] Australian Institute of Marine Science 2018, "Long-term reef monitoring program - Annual summary report on coral reef condition for 2017/2018", Downloaded on October 23, 2018 from https://www.aims.gov.au/reef-monitoring/gbr-condition-summary-2017-2018

that with business-as-usual increases of carbon dioxide in the atmosphere, 99% of coral reefs will die off by 2100.[52]

*Plastic in the oceans.* Plastic in the ocean may seem like a coastal issue, but it is not. Around 90% of plastic pollution in the ocean can be traced to inland rivers.[53] Through these waterways, as well as coastal and on-water plastic sources, 4.8 million metric tons of plastic were deposited into the ocean in the year 2010, that's 10,560,000,000 pounds of plastic finding its way into the ocean, annually.[54] Put yet another way, that's about one garbage truck full of plastic every minute. The vast majority of ALL plastic debris ends up in the ocean, including ⅓ of all plastic packaging ever produced. With a business-as-usual trajectory, the amount of plastic in the ocean is expected to double by 2030 and to quadruple by 2050, at which point plastics will outweigh fish in the seas. This pollution is estimated to cause 13 billion US dollars of marine ecosystem damage per year.[55] Around 80% of ocean litter is plastic, and much of that is from single-use packaging -- straws and plastic water bottles, grocery bags, and food containers dominate the mess.

Where does all this plastic which we dump into the ocean go? All over the ocean. Plastic has been found on the remotest islands, on the ocean floor, in mid-ocean plastic garbage patches larger than most countries,[56,57] in the guts of many marine

---

[52] von Hooidonk, R. et al. 2016 "Local-scale projections of coral reef futures and implactions of the Paris Agreement", Scientific Reports 6, Article number 39666

[53] Schmidt, C. et al 2017, "Export of plastic debris by rivers into the sea", Environ. Sci. Technol. 2017, 51, 21, 12246-12253

[54] UNEP 2016, "Marine plastic debris and microplastics - Global issues and research to inspire action and policy change", United Nations Environment Programme, Nairobi

[55] World Economic Forum 2016, Ellen MacArthur Foundation and McKinsey & Company, The New Plastics Economy-Rethinking the future of plastics http://www.ellenmacarthurfoundation.org/publications

[56] Lebreton, L. et al 2018 "Evidence that the Great Pacific Garbage Patch is rapidly accumulating plastic",*Scientific Reports* **8**, Article number: 4666

[57] https://en.wikipedia.org/wiki/List_of_countries_and_dependencies_by_area accessed May 25, 2019

organisms, and even in Arctic ice.[58] The impacts of macroplastics, which are defined to be larger than 0.2 inches / 5 mm, include ingestion by and entanglement of fish, mammals, and birds, as well as direct damage to ocean ecosystems. Eighty percent of seabirds have plastic in their stomachs. North Sea gulls have an average of 30 pieces of plastic in their stomachs. 10% of the contents of the stomach of the lantern fish, a primary food source for tuna, is plastic. All 1.5 million Laysan albatrosses are believed to have plastic in their digestive systems. A whale who died off the coast of Norway was found to have 30 plastic bags in its belly. Plastic can strangle or choke the animals, or if it makes it into the stomach of the animal, it can lead to malnutrition, starvation, and death. Furthermore, exposure to plasticizers can lead to developmental defects, particularly to hormonal systems.[59]

How long will this macroplastic last in the environment? Longer than the 50 years plastic has been around for sure, but how long, we don't know. Most plastics don't biodegrade at all because the bacteria which drive biodegradation don't recognize plastics as food. However, plastic does *photo*degrade. This means photons, or light, breaks bonds in the long molecular strings found in plastic, shortening the molecular strings. Estimates are that it will take about 500 years for your standard grocery store plastic bag or water bottle to fully degrade.

However, degradation does not mean the plastic is gone, rather that it is no longer visible to the human eye. Macroplastics degrade into smaller pieces called microplastics, bits smaller than 5mm / 0.2 inches. Microplastics also come from abrasion of automobile tires, washing of synthetic fibers in our washing machines, and the production of many cosmetics. We do not know the full health implications of microplastics yet. Still, we know they are far-ranging including hormonal system damage to causing cancers. When small enough, microplastics are known to cross

---

58 UNEP 2016, "Marine plastic debris and microplastics - Global issues and research to inspire action and policy change", United Nations Environment Programme, Nairobi

59 Plastic pollution, 30 October 2018, Wikipedia https://en.wikipedia.org/wiki/Plastic_pollution#cite_note-Plastic_Pollution-5

cell membranes into various organs such as the brain and the placenta, where they can cause developmental problems[60].

Worryingly, microplastics have been found everywhere, including in the urine of 95% of adults in the US[61], and in many commercial fish and shellfish species.[62] Ninety percent of bottled water and most tap water contains microplastic.[63] The current levels of microplastics in water and food are below levels believed to be of concern to human health. Although, I question the influence of the $300 billion plastic packaging industry[64] on this conclusion. And of course, there is far more microplastic in the pipeline as all our macroplastic litter degrades. While there are many unanswered questions about plastic waste, there is enough evidence that the UN has urged invoking the precautionary approach with regard to plastic. In other words, we should address plastic waste problems before it starts drastically harming us and wildlife.[65]

*Warming oceans and sea level rise.* Since 1900 the ocean surface temperature has risen 1.4°F / 0.7°C. We expect a whooping 4.9°F / 2.7°C rise in ocean surface temperatures by the

---

[60] UNEP (2016). Marine plastic debris and microplastics – Global lessons and research to inspire action and guide policy change. United Nations Environment Programme, Nairobi.

[61] North, Emily J.; Halden, Rolf U. (1 January 2013). "Plastics and environmental health: the road ahead". *Reviews on Environmental Health*. **28** (1): 1–8. doi:10.1515/reveh-2012-0030. PMC 3791860. PMID 23337043.

[62] UNEP (2016). Marine plastic debris and microplastics – Global lessons and research to inspire action and guide policy change. United Nations Environment Programme, Nairobi.

[63] Mason, S.A. et al 2018, "Synthetic polymer contamination in bottled water", downloaded from https://orbmedia.org/sites/default/files/FinalBottledWaterReport.pdf on October 31, 2018. (note this particular study was not peer reviewed but has been subsequently referenced by experts in the field)

[64] Transparency Market Research 2015, Plastic packaging market - Global industry analysis, size, share, growth, trends and forecast 2014-2020, Snapshot accessed October 31, 2018 at https://www.transparencymarketresearch.com/plastic-packaging.html

[65] UNEP 2016 "Marine Plastic Debris & Microplastics - Global lessons and research to inspire action and guide policy change" United Nations Environment Programme, Nairobi

end of 2100 with very high confidence.[66] Rising ocean temperatures drive the expansion of ocean water and are estimated to be responsible for 42% of the observed 3 inches / 8 cm of sea level rise observed since 1900, the remainder of sea level rise is due to melting glaciers. With the continuing increase of ocean temperatures, we expect a sea level rise of 2 - 8 feet / 0.6 - 2.7 meters by the end of the century. If the Antarctic ice sheet melts, sea level will rise by a whooping 180 feet / 56 meters.[67] Sea level rise has drastic impacts on coastal and island cities and farms, including flooding, salinization of freshwater supplies, and increased numbers of refugees seeking dry ground.

Increased ocean temperatures are also likely to lead to a shifting of ocean circulation patterns, which influence rainfall patterns and temperature on land. For example, although London is at the same latitude as subarctic land-locked Irkutsk, London's climate is quite mild. This difference in temperature is largely due to London's proximity to the ocean and the relatively warm waters of the Gulf Stream transporting equatorial heat northward.

Finally, as ocean temperatures increase, we expect more evaporation as sunlight energy converts liquid water into vapor. When that water condenses back into liquid, it releases heat, which is indeed what powers hurricanes. Thus warmer oceans lead to more intense hurricanes. There is evidence that this is already happening. Research shows that the most expensive hurricane season in America, 2017, which cost $200 billion in damages,[68] was driven by above average Atlantic temperatures.[69]

---

[66] IPCC?

[67] Wikipedia and references therein, https://en.wikipedia.org/wiki/Sea_level_rise, accessed November 4, 2018

[68] https://news.nationalgeographic.com/2017/11/2017-hurricane-season-most-expensive-us-history-spd/ accessed July 15, 2019

[69] Murakami, H. et al., 2018 "Dominant effect of relative tropical Atlantic warming on major hurricane occurrence", Science, doi/10.1126/science.aat6711

## III. Clean freshwater

Water, of course, is essential for plant and animal life, including humans. Indeed, the United Nations (UN) lists access to clean drinking water as one of its 17 sustainable development goals to transform the world.[70] Rivers, lakes, and wetlands provide water regulation, prevent floods and release water in dry spells, provide water cleaning functions, act as a natural transport system, and are unique ecosystems in their own right. There are two main ways in which humanity is negatively influencing the health of the planet's freshwater: through changing the flow of water and through pollution. In the *Planetary Wheel* fiigure, I present three measures of how we have impacted the flow of freshwater because these are easier to calculate than a fractional pollution impact. But don't doubt that having clean water is just as critical as having ample freshwater. I discuss both aspects below.

As noted above, humanity extracts roughly 65% of the freshwater that we can without causing regime change to aquatic water systems.[71] 48% of all river volume is currently moderately to severely impacted by dams or is fragmented. If all planned dams are built, only 7% of the world's rivers will continue to flow naturally.[72] Changes in flow have contributed dramatically to the drop of 41% of river and 39% of wetland vertebrates between 1970 to 2012.[73] 87% of wetlands have disappeared since the 1700s, and their loss rate is accelerating with 30% of this decline in the last 40 years alone.[74] Recent studies estimate that 47% of large cities and 71% of irrigated areas experience water

---

[70] https://www.un.org/sustainabledevelopment/ accessed July 2, 2019

[71] Steffen, W. et al, 2015, "Planetary boundaries: guiding human development on a changing planet", Science Express Jan 15, 2015, 10.1126/science.1259855

[72] Günther Grill et al, 2015, "An index-based framework for assessing patterns and trends in river fragmentation and flow regulation by global dams at multiple scales", *Environ. Res. Lett.* **10** 015001

[73] WWF. 2016. Living Planet Report 2016. Risk and resilience in a new era. WWF International, Gland, Switzerland

[74] Ramsar Convention on Wetlands, 2018, *Global Wetland Outlook: State of the World's Wetlands and their Services to People.* Gland, Switzerland: Ramsar Convention Secretariat.

shortages.[75] Some 70% of water withdrawals are for agriculture, which in turn is dominated by water withdrawals for livestock[76]. The Office of the Director of National Intelligence has predicted that water will become the new oil in terms of political alliances and unrest.[77]

And what about the water that remains in the rivers and lakes? Direct dumping and runoff can disrupt natural cycles or poison water ecosystems. Runoff laden with fertilizers or fecal matter, primarily from livestock farms, can result in nutrient dumps into the water. Nutrient loading can lead to an algal bloom, which uses up all the oxygen in the water, choking the indigenous creatures. This process, known as eutrophication, costs the U.S. about 2.2 billion USD every year in costs to revive ecosystems and clean up drinking water, and loss of real estate value and recreational use in freshwater systems alone.[78] Runoff from agricultural fields also can contain large amounts of pesticides, which have been known to drive high rates of fish mortality.[79] As for chemical waste, the National Geographic Society has estimated that 70% of industrial wastes are dumped untreated into waterways in developing countries[80]. The list of industrial pollutant sources is frighteningly long. Here are just a few: textiles, sugar and paper industries, medical treatments, power plants, and paint and varnish production and disposal. The pollutants include plastics, oils, greases, and metallic waste like copper, arsenic,

---

[75] Brauman, K. et al 2016, "Water depletion: an improved metric for incorporating seasonal and dry-year water scarcity into water risk assessments" *Elementa: Science of the Anthropocene* • 4: 000083 • doi: 10.12952/journal.elementa.000083

[76] Food and Agriculture Organization of the UN (FAO) 2006, "Livestock's long shadow", ISBN 978-92-5-105571-7

[77] Office of the Director of National Intelligence, USA 2012, "Global water security", Intelligence community assessment ICA 2012-08

[78] Dodds, W. Et al 2009 "Eutrophication in U.S. Freshwaters: Analysis of Potential Economic Damages", ENVIRONMENTAL SCIENCE & TECHNOLOGY / VOL. 43, NO. 1, 2009

[79] Helfrich, LA, Weigmann, DL, Hipkins, P, and Stinson, ER (June 1996), Pesticides and aquatic animals: A guide to reducing impacts on aquatic systems. Virginia Cooperative Extension. Retrieved on 2007-10-14.

[80] https://www.nationalgeographic.com/environment/freshwater/pollution/ accessed May 16, 2019

mercury, acids, chlorides, and zinc. I discuss some of these more in the Toxicant Free section below.

## IV. Toxicant free environment

I include a toxicant free environment as a separate resource because it highlights human and ecosystem vulnerabilities to poisons. In contrast, the other seven natural resources are broadly large-scale physical chunks of the earth-fresh and saltwater, soil, life, land, climate, and air. A toxicant free environment overlaps with these, of course, in particular with fresh water and air. For instance, the World Health Organization (WHO) estimates that 22% of all deaths, in the year 2012, could have been prevented if modifiable environmental factors were removed. These include reducing air pollution, occupational risks, overexposure to toxicants, ultraviolet radiation, noise, contaminated water, and so forth.[81] In the following, I have focused on two instances of pollution: toxic waste and pesticides.

The organizations Pure Earth and Green Cross provided a useful summary of the scale of the toxic waste problem. They note that there are over 150,000 sites globally, which they identified as toxic sites with an estimated 200,000,000 people at risk.[82] Toxic waste causes both acute and long-term problems with approximately one in five cases of cancer associated with environmental exposures.[83] In addition to shortened life spans, toxic chemicals can also reduce the quality of life and the ability to work. Pure Earth and Green Cross estimated toxic pollution leads to 17 million disability-adjusted life years (DALYs) annually. One DALY represents the loss of one year of healthy life, including both years lost to premature death and debilitating health. The

---

[81] Prüss-Ustün, A., J. Wolf, C. Corvalán, R. Bos and M. Neira 2016, Preventing disease through
healthy environments: A global assessment of the burden of disease from environmental risks. World Health Organization.

[82] Green Cross Switzerland and Pure Earth 2016, *The World's Worst Pollution Problems 2016: The Toxics Beneath Our Feet*

[83] Vineis P, Xun W. The emerging epidemic of environmental cancers in developing countries. *Annals of Oncology*. 2008;20(2):205-212.

magnitude of DALYs attributable to toxic waste is similar to the public health impact of malaria or tuberculosis. The 10 largest industrial sources of DALYs are lead-acid battery recycling (2-4.8 million DALYs), mining and ore processing (0.45-2.6 million), lead smelting (1-2.5million), tanneries (1.2- 2 million), small scale gold mining (0.6-1.6 million), industrial dumpsites (0.37-1.2 million), industrial estates (0.37 - 1.2 million), chemical manufacturing (0.3-0.75 million), product manufacturing (0.4-0.7 million), and the dye industry (0.22 - 0.43 million).[84]

Unlike toxic waste sites, which are often "hot spots", pesticides are a widespread toxicant. These include the application of herbicides, fungicides, and insecticides. A recent UN report summarized that pesticides have "catastrophic impacts on the environment, human health, and society as a whole." The report states on the order of 200,000 deaths a year are due to short-term acute exposure to pesticides with horrific examples of dozens of children dying en masse from eating contaminated food. Whereas longer term chronic exposure is linked to cancer, Alzheimers and Parkinsons, hormone disruption, developmental disorders, sterility, higher rates of miscarriage and birth-defects, memory loss, loss of coordination, reduced sight, and motor skills. Again, there are many disturbing examples of communities near agricultural land with increased rates of sterility, cancer, tuberculosis, and skin diseases, and impacts on children's intellectual development, as well as behavioral and developmental issues.[85]. Recently, courts have found in favor of farmers suing Monsanto for health impacts, the makers of the weedkiller

---

[84] Green Cross Switzerland and Pure Earth 2016, *The World's Worst Pollution Problems 2016: The Toxics Beneath Our Feet*

[85] UN Human Rights Council 2017, *Report of the Special Rapporteur on the Right to Food,* A/HRC/34/48, Downloaded on October 10, 2018 from https://ap.ohchr.org/documents/dpage_e.aspx?m=101
Or https://documents-dds-ny.un.org/doc/UNDOC/GEN/G17/017/85/PDF/G1701785.pdf?OpenElement

Roundup, awarding 2 billion US dollars to a couple in Oakland[86] and $80 million to a man in San Francisco.[87]

It is not only the people working on farms or living near them who are impacted. Pesticide residues are very prevalent in plant and animal foods, with 70% of US produce found to have pesticide residue on it even after washing. The most commonly detected pesticide in food, Dacthal, also known as DCPA , was banned in the EU in 2009[88] and listed as a possible carcinogen in the US.[89] Animals, on land and in the water, can accumulate pesticides over their lifetime and may represent a dangerous vector of poisons for human consumption. The most famous example of so-called bioaccumulation may be mercury accumulation in fish.[90]

And of course, it is not only human health which is impacted, for pesticides disrupt ecosystems both in the location of application and downwind or downstream. The consequent reductions in 'pest' populations of native plants and animals upsets predator-prey balances within the food chain and can destabilize ecosystems. Undoubtedly, the poisons also impact the health of the surviving insects and plants, making them less resilient to other stresses such as habitat fragmentation or non-native invasive species. The neonicotinoid pesticides have been

---

[86]https://www.cbsnews.com/news/jury-awards-couple-2billion-monsanto-roundup-weed-killer-cancer-lawsuit-trial-today-2019-05-13/ accessed May 19, 2019

[87]https://www.theguardian.com/business/2019/apr/11/french-court-finds-monsanto-guilty-of-poisoning-farmer accessed May 19, 2019

[88] Vassiliou, A, for the European Commision 2009, "Commission decision of 23 September 2009 concerning the non-inclusion of chlorthal-dimethyl in Annex I to Council Directive 91/414/EEC and the withdrawal of authorisations for plant protection products containing that substance", Offiial Journal of the European Commission 24.09.2009

[89] Environmental Protection Agency 2018, "Chemicals evaluated for carcinogenic potential annual cancer report 2018"
Holden, E. "Pesticide residues found in 70% of produce sold in US even after washing", *The Guardian*

[90] UN Human Rights Council 2017, *Report of the Special Rapporteur on the Right to Food*, Downloaded on October 10, 2018 from https://documents-dds-ny.un.org/doc/UNDOC/GEN/G17/017/85/PDF/G1701785.pdf?OpenElement

## We don't need pesticides to feed humanity

**To feed one person organically**

*Allotments in the UK are 1/16 of an acre and were designed to feed a family of 4. One person needs 1/64 of an acre.*

**To feed 7.6 billion people**

*0.118 billion acres to feed humanity organically*

**Currently 3.7 billion acres farmed**

*According to the UN, pesticide free farming can easily feed the world with healthier, more nutrient rich food. The UN concludes that world hunger arises because of poverty and distribution problems, not production issues.* FAO 2019, www.fao.org/faostat

implicated as one of the contributing causes to the dramatic drop observed in honey bee colonies. There are wildly varying reports of the importance of bees for crop production depending on how the question is framed. For clarity, I consulted a comprehensive review which concluded that 42% of the top 57 crops are pollinated, at least in part, by wild bees and that certain crops, such as many nuts and coffee, are reliant on honey bee pollination.[91] Given the economic importance of bees, there has been a great deal of research on the impact of neonicotinoids, a common pesticide, on bees. The research has led to different conclusions.[92] However, after careful consideration many countries decided to ban the use of some neonicotinoids, notably

---

91 Klein, A.M. et al 2007, "*Importance of pollinators in changing landscapes for world crops*", Proceedings of the Royal Society B, 273, 303

92 https://en.wikipedia.org/wiki/Neonicotinoid accessed May 22, 2020

the EU banned 3 varieties in 2013.[93] Pesticide use is also a critical factor in the catastrophic reduction in other insect numbers being documented at sites around the world, see the biodiversity section below.

The multi-faceted benefits of food grown without pesticides then include improving one's health, protecting farmworkers and nearby communities, giving honey bees and other critters a fighting chance, and reducing poison in the environment. But the pesticide industry would have you believe that we can not grow enough food organically to feed the world. That is a downright lie. Luckily this one is easy enough to counter: see the box "We don't need pesticides to feed humanity". My simple calculation scales up the size of a British allotment to estimate the amount of land needed to feed the world. Allotments were designed to provide enough land to feed a family of four, organically, during the crunch of World War II. If we allocate an allotment worth of land for every four people on the planet, we would need only 1/30 of the currently farmed land to feed everyone, organically. Of course, allotments don't account for meat or out of season produce, but if we use the old adage that 10 times as much land is needed to produce meat protein as veg protein, and we all ate only meat, we'd need 10 allotments per 4 people, or ⅓ of the area currently farmed to feed ourselves, organically.

It is not only my simplified calculation which denounces the myth that pesticides are necessary to feed the world. A 2018 United Nations (UN) report also concludes that without pesticides, we can produce plenty of food. Indeed, the report states we can produce healthier and more nutrient-rich food, on fields with higher yield in the long run, if we return to organic practices. According to the UN, the problem with world hunger is not about food production, but about poverty and distribution.

So why would the pesticide industry want us to believe pesticides are essential? Could it be linked to the market value of pesticides of 50 billion US dollars a year? The UN notes that the

---

[93] European Commission, "Pesticides: Approval of Active Substances: Neonicotinoids"
https://ec.europa.eu/food/plant/pesticides/approval_active_substances/approval_renewal/neonicotinoids_en accessed May 22, 2020

pesticide industry has engaged in a "systematic denial of harms", "aggressive and unethical marketing tactics" and "heavy lobbying of governments".[94,95] These actions have led to the blockage of reforms and restrictions in pesticide use. Sounds remarkably like the tobacco industry in the 1970s. But wait, analogies to the tobacco industry have already been claimed by those fighting for clean air and climate change.[96] Hmm... seems to be a lot of that going around.

And this story of healthy bountiful returns from reducing the use of toxic pollutants is repeated in other sectors as well. The Lancet Commission on Pollution and Health provides a comprehensive analysis of patterns in pollution, their impacts, and the efficacy of pollution control. As noted previously, for every dollar invested in air pollution control, there are $30 in benefits. The removal of lead from gasoline has been estimated to be worth 6 billion dollars to the US economy through the enhanced cognitive function, and therefore productivity, of generations of children. Many win/win solutions to reduce toxic pollutants exist, but companies apparently need to have economic incentives to enact them. Otherwise it can be cheaper for the company to pollute. Of course, this costs us more in the long run as we pay for clean up and health care, not to mention the financial and other costs of the degradation of the environment.

## V. Stable climate

Part of me wishes I could leave out this section altogether, for I don't want to alienate people who are tired of hearing about climate change. Perhaps you think it is all lies made up by

---

[94] https://www.theguardian.com/environment/2017/mar/07/un-experts-denounce-myth-pesticides-are-necessary-to-feed-the-world

[95] UN Human Rights Council 2017, *Report of the Special Rapporteur on the Right to Food*, A/HRC/34/48, Accessed on December 29, 2019 https://documents-dds-ny.un.org/doc/UNDOC/GEN/G17/017/85/pdf/G1701785.pdf?OpenElement

[96] https://www.theguardian.com/commentisfree/2018/oct/27/air-pollution-is-the-new-tobacco-time-to-tackle-this-epidemic

scientists to earn money or some other scheme perpetrated for nefarious ends. My assurances to the contrary are unlikely to sway you, and by discussing climate change I risk offending you. However, a stable climate is an essential natural resource if we want the current set of life on the planet to survive and thrive. It would be irresponsible to neglect it.

A stable climate is hugely beneficial to us and wildlife because, for starters, rainfall and temperature patterns along with soil are the primary factors determining what form vegetation will take. This includes the distribution of natural ecosystems such as grasslands and forests, as well as crop choices. As climate changes, plant and animal ranges shift, exposing them to new challenges such as transportation issues to track the optimum climate, new competitors, a different mix of predators and food sources, different pests, and different diseases. And for farmers, shifting weather means difficulty in planning when, what and how to plant to maximize yields.

Even in a relatively stable climate, ecosystems continually change and farmers adjust their practices in response to changing local weather conditions. However, it appears that the current rates of climate change exceed those previously experienced, making adaptation and planning difficult.

In addition to changing rainfall and temperature patterns, severe weather is increasing. Some of the consequences of this are more flooding, shifting disease ranges, and more wilderness fires. Civilization has developed around current weather patterns. Cities are built on areas above sea level, farms are built where the soil and weather produce good yields. As weather patterns and sea-levels shift, people will be on the move to secure the resources they need to live. Already we see some climate change induced migration, and much more is expected. Furthermore, It is very likely that without a drastic reduction in carbon emissions, ecosystems will collapse in the coming decades. For instance, higher latitudes are warming more quickly than temperate and equatorial ones, and the permafrost in arctic tundra is beginning to melt. This melting will lead to the emission of vast amounts of the potent greenhouse gas methane and will accelerate warming -

one of the reasons we aim to keep global warming below 1.5°C (2.7°F)[97].

I will not go into a detailed discussion here of how we know that humans are causing climate change; plenty has been written on this. But I can refer you to the horse's mouth as it were. Every seven or eight years, a broad international, inter-institutional group of 100s, if not 1000s, of researchers and policy makers painstakingly review the state of climate change research and policy. This group of authors are collectively known as the IPPC, the Intergovernmental Panel on Climate Change and anyone may access their reports and summaries for free online in a variety of languages.[98] Alternatively, one can reference the US government's 2017 report on climate change. Both reports summarize the many observations which support the tenant that human emissions are driving climate change. Most famous amongst these observations is the global temperature record.

Multiple datasets show that the last 17 years of the 1880 - 2016 record included 16 of the hottest years since instrumental records began, with 2014, 2015, and 2016 each subsequently breaking the hottest year records. Data after 2016 weren't available at the time of the US summary report. A more recent study, by NASA, finds that of the hottest 20 years since regords began in 1984, 19 were between the years 2001 and 2019. I show this as 5% in the Planetary Wheel figure to represent the 1 year out of the 20 years that is not in the top 120 hottest years in the 140 year record. The global average temperature in recent decades (1986-2016) is 1.2°F / 0.7°C hotter than in the 60 years between 1901-1960 - considered as 'pre-industrial' in climate studies. Additionally, oceans are getting warmer, sea-level is rising, the troposphere is getting warmer, and snow cover and sea ice are both decreasing. None of these trends can be accounted for by natural variability, volcanoes, or solar variability. Only human-induced climate change explains the trends and the

---

[97] IPCC, 2018: Summary for Policymakers. In: *Global Warming of 1.5°C.*

[98] Intergoverental Panel on Climate Change 2014, *Synthesis Report. Contribution of Working Groups I, II and III to the Fifth Assessment Report of the Intergovernmental Panel on Climate Change*, IPCC, Geneva, Switzerland, 151 pp.

complex patterns seen across the globe. With concerted and strong action, we can keep the global temperature increase at or below 2.7°F (1.5°C), the agreed 'safe' target, by the end of the century. Without ***major*** reductions in emissions, the global average temperature will rise on the order of 9°F (5°C), by the end of the century.[99]

Here are some facts to consider if you still don't believe human's carbon emissions are driving climate change:

- The underlying principles linking the rise in greenhouse gases to rising temperatures are elementary physics and were known in the 1870s. It is the same principle as putting a blanket over you to stay warm. Heat that normally would have escaped as infra-red radiation, bounces off the blanket/atmosphere to make you warmer. We understand the greenhouse effect well from two compelling examples. First, the greenhouse effect warms the Earth enough to make it habitable. Second, the greenhouse effect explains why Venus has surface temperatures exceeding 800°F. It is because Venus has a great deal of carbon dioxide in its atmosphere.
- 197 of 199 countries are confident enough that our emissions are driving climate change that they have committed to reducing emissions. The two countries which have not are Syria and Nicaragua. The US government has now stated they will be exiting the agreement.[100]
- There are ongoing and increasing signs of a destabilized climate. There is more water in the atmosphere, melting polar and alpine ice, earlier bud burst, higher temperature

---

[99] Wuebbles, D.J., D.W. Fahey, K.A. Hibbard, B. DeAngelo, S. Doherty, K. Hayhoe, R. Horton, J.P. Kossin, P.C. Taylor, A.M. Waple, and C.P. Weaver, 2017: Executive summary. In: Climate Science Special Report: Fourth National Climate Assessment, Volume I [Wuebbles, D.J., D.W. Fahey, K.A. Hibbard, D.J. Dokken, B.C. Stewart, and T.K. Maycock (eds.)]. U.S. Global Change Research Program, Washington, DC, USA, pp. 12-34, doi: 10.7930/J0DJ5CTG.

[100] Accessed July 15, 2019 https://en.wikipedia.org/wiki/List_of_parties_to_the_Paris_Agreement#Non-signatories

records, more droughts, rising sea-level, and an increased spread of diseases.[101]

- Divestment in fossil fuels is vast and growing - trillions of dollars of investment have been removed from carbon-intensive companies by thousands of organizations including the World Council of Churches and insurance companies such as Axa and Allianz.[102,103]
- Exxon has known about climate change since the 1980s. Eighty percent of Exxon's internal papers acknowledge climate change is real.[104]

But perhaps more persuasive is the age-old adage 'Better safe than sorry'. With so much of the world convinced climate change is a real and present danger, we should at least consider the possibility that it is real. And if it is possibly happening, it would be irresponsible not to change our actions. When taken together with the many positive aspects of reducing greenhouse gas emissions, such as reducing ocean acidification, increasing energy security, cleaner air, and new technological markets, why not strive to reduce our emissions?

## VI. Wild land

Why should we care about wilderness? For me, wilderness and the creatures that live there are inherently worthy of respect. But even if you believe that wilderness exists simply for

---

[101] The Intergovernmental Panel on Climate Change 2014- The synthesis report. https://www.ipcc.ch/report/ar5/syr/

[102] Guardian article, McKibben, B, Dec 16, 2018, "At last, divestment is hitting the fossil fuel industry where it hurts" https://www.theguardian.com/commentisfree/2018/dec/16/divestment-fossil-fuel-industry-trillions-dollars-investments-carbon

[103]https://www.theguardian.com/commentisfree/2018/jan/11/new-york-city-oil-industry-war-divestment

[104]https://www.theguardian.com/environment/2015/jul/08/exxon-climate-change-1981-climate-denier-funding and https://www.theguardian.com/environment/climate-consensus-97-per-cent/2017/aug/23/harvard-scientists-took-exxons-challenge-found-it-using-the-tobacco-playbook

humanity's use, the loss of wilderness runs smack into the heart of most modern religions, especially Christianity. Large numbers of humanity already suffer significantly from environmental degradation driven by humanity's consumption patterns. And if we don't stop the destruction of wilderness, many many more people will experience consequent water and food shortages, natural disasters, and disease. Indeed, it is now generally accepted by aid organizations, that to lift the world's poor out of poverty requires environmental protection and to protect the environment requires alleviating poverty.

The poorest of us rely directly on the wilderness for our food, fuel, shelter, and livelihoods. When natural resources are depleted, those without financial resources are much more likely to be unable to collect food or to earn a living. Thus environmental degradation becomes a social justice issue as our consumption patterns deplete the quality of other people's lives. But of course, those with more financial wealth also rely on a robust wilderness for clean air and water, for climate stability enabling agriculture, and for fuel and shelter. Furthermore, wilderness is essential as a buffer against natural disasters such as floods, and the impact of climate change.[105] Finally, wilderness holds unknowable opportunities for medicines, food, fibers, genetic diversity, wonder, and spiritual well-being, amongst other economic and social resources. To ensure future generations have adaptation options, the wilderness must remain large and healthy. Thus saving the wilderness is essential for intergenerational justice, as well as social justice today.

There are about 149 million square kilometers (57 million square miles) of land on the globe, excluding the Antarctic, rock, and ice covered land and lakes. These 149,000,000 square kilometers of so-called arable land include all the area available for farming, housing, roads, manufacturing, energy, plants, and so forth.[106] What proportion of this land do you think should be left for the other millions of species living on the planet? Do you have a

---

105 UNDP-UNEP Poverty-Environment Initiative 2015, Mainstreaming environment and climate for poverty reduction and sustainable development, available online at www.unpei.org.

106 Wikipedia, https://en.wikipedia.org/wiki/Land accessed June 3, 2019

percentage in mind? You may wish to increase that percentage when you recognize that in order for ecosystems to thrive and function well, they need to be quite large. Big areas are needed to facilitate migration and repopulation, so ecosystems and species can withstand disease, invasive species, and changing food webs or weather.

Researchers have estimated that at least 50% of the land surface should be retained as wilderness to ensure its resiliency. The idea that 'Nature Needs Half' has been around since the 1970s and is also the conclusion of more recent studies that analyze extinction rates relative to the area of natural habitat.[107, 108] Furthermore, given our current lack of a deep understanding of how ecosystems function, 50% seems like a minimal amount to grant the 7,000,000, at least, nonhuman species on the planet. Remember that this 50% of land to others will be what makes life possible for the one species contemplating this allocation, humans. I'd argue for 80 or 90% for other species since humans are only one species of many millions.

Currently, about 15% of the global arable land area has protected status of one kind or another.[109] Protected areas are not all "given over" to wild beings. Some protected areas are logged, some are open for recreation, and some are used for traditional hunting and gathering. But in protected areas these activities are managed to ensure wildlife can thrive. We could expand the 15% of protected land to 23% by including all the places on the planet that are still wild, included as a slice in the Wild lands section of the *Planetary Wheel* figure[110]. And we could readily reach the target of 50% of arable land being protected, if we redesigned how we eat and raise meat. Meat production currently uses a shocking 59% of arable land, composed of 26%

---

[107] Locke, H. 2013, "Nature needs half: a necessary and hopeful new agenda for protected areas", Parks vol 19

[108] Wilson, E.O. 2016, Half-Earth: Our Planet's Fight for Life. Liveright

[109] Juffe-Bignoli, D, et al. (2014). Protected Planet Report 2014. Cambridge (UK): UNEP World Conservation Monitoring Centre

[110] Watson et al., 2016, "Catastrophic declines in wilderness areas undermine global environment targets", Current Biology 26, 2929–2934 November 7, Elsevier Ltd. http://dx.doi.org/10.1016/j.cub.2016.08.049

of the global arable land surface used for grazing and 33% for raising feed[111]. As a final note on wilderness land area, in the last two decades we have lost about 1.3 million square miles (3.3 million square kilometers) of wilderness representing approximately 1/10 of global wilderness. This loss of wilderness is about twice the area that was given protected status over the same time period.

Another way to look at how much wilderness is left is to look at the status of different biomes. Biomes are global ecosystems delineated by their variation in structure and seasonality, thus harboring different plants and animals. Examples are tundra, a treeless, highly seasonal ecosystem, and tropical rainforests, with multi-layered tree canopies in a climate that varies little over the year. According to a study by Watson, there are 14 global biomes. Three of these no longer have any large wilderness blocks. A further five biomes have less than 10% of their original extent remaining.[112]

Eco-footprint analyses of available wilderness won't make you feel any better. Eco-footprints are an attempt to quantify how much land is needed to support a human's life. This includes the food one eats, the energy one uses, and the stuff one buys. Eco-footprints also account for the safe disposal of any waste created and the replenishment of resources by our activities. Using eco-footprints, researchers can estimate how much land would be needed if everyone on earth lived like the average American. A world full of American consumers would need over five Earths to supply the necessary resources and absorb the waste created. Americans' average is about three times the global average. And every year. All together, humanity needs about 1.7 Earths worth of resources to produce, replenish, and safely dispose of the resources we use. What does it mean that these estimates are greater than one?

---

[111] Food and Agriculture Organization of the UN (FAO) 2006, "Livestock's long shadow", ISBN 978-92-5-105571-7

[112] Watson et al., 2016, "Catastrophic declines in wilderness areas undermine global environment targets", Current Biology 26, 2929–2934 November 7, Elsevier Ltd. http://dx.doi.org/10.1016/j.cub.2016.08.049

A global eco-footprint higher than one Earth implies that the rate at which we are using up resources is faster than the rate at which ecosystems regenerate those resources. For example, we are depleting the soil faster than it is created. We can make an analogy with a bank account and that when our eco-footprint is one or less, we are living off the interest of the earth's capital. When our eco-footprint exceeds one, we are depleting our bank account balance and eating into our natural capital. Not a viable long-term plan. Because the global eco-footprint does exceed one Earth, we need to reduce our consumption to regain a long-term viable society. I've displayed the eco-footprint estimate of remaining wilderness as a 0% on the Planetary Resource Wheel because we have no safe way to expand our consumption. Note, that without any significant change to lifestyles, Americans could halve their footprints to the level of Brits and Europeans, who average about 2.6 Earths, without any undue hardship.[113] However, we should probably still aim to reduce our footprints to one or less for fairness sake.

## VII. Biodiversity

Separate from wildlands, but closely related, is the resource of biodiversity - the abundance and diversity of life. Biodiversity includes genetic diversity, species diversity, and diversity in ecosystems. It is becoming more clear that our understanding of how organisms in an ecosystem interact is woefully primitive. For instance, our definition of species, being able to reproduce viable offspring, turns out to be a human construct - albeit an extremely useful one in the field of biology. Amongst this uncertainty, however, we do have certainty that diversity underpins the ability to survive under changing circumstances.

Variety gives life the option of using different strategies to respond to crises. This is true whether the disturbance is deforestation, changing predator/prey/food circumstances or chemical cycles, climate shifts, or pollution stresses. Individuals

[113] Global Footprint Network 2016, https://www.footprintnetwork.org/ accessed July 15, 2019

who survive a disaster can repopulate not only their local communities but also neighboring areas where their species may have been wiped out. Considering biodiversity as a resource in its own right assures that we protect a medley of grasslands, forests, and deserts for years to come. Each ecosystem, each living being, is unique. Any one of them may prove critical for the survival of a species or ecosystem in the years to come.

How do we measure biodiversity and thus estimate its current status? In the past, scientists have used species counts, the number of existing species in a given area, and species extinctions to document biodiversity. However, complete species loss is an extreme case that neglects the loss of genetic and ecosystem diversity as well as the robustness or fragility of existing populations. Local and, even more so, global extinctions are drastic results, typically following prolonged population declines. Nonetheless, even these extreme events of species extinctions tell a frightening tale. The usual background rate of extinction in the geological record is estimated to be about one vertebrate (animal with a spine) extinction every 50 or 100 years. In the last 100 years, over 200 vertebrates have gone extinct. That is 100-200 times greater than the background rate.[114] According to the planetary boundary study, such an extinction rate is beyond tour safe operating space and is thus shown as 0% on the *Planetary Wheel* figure.[115]

Some groups of living beings are more susceptible to extinction than others. For instance, 41% of frog species are threatened with extinction. Frankly, we do not know the ecological implications of the loss of individual species. I feel it is an incalculable loss for an entire species to die out. However, as noted above, extinction is the dramatic end point of losses of populations and shrinking of geographical range. Therefore, scientists are now turning to other measures of biodiversity - notably counts of individuals.

---

[114] Ceballos G, et al. (2015) Accelerated modern human-induced species losses: Entering the sixth mass extinction. Sci Adv 1:e1400253.

[115] Steffen, W. et al, 2015, “Planetary boundaries: guiding human development on a changing planet”, Science Express Jan 15, 2015, 10.1126/science.1259855

The World Wildlife Fund has been studying the issue of dwindling numbers of wild animals by monitoring a staggering 3,706 animal species from 1970 to the present day. It is a chilling story. Between 1970 and 2012, more than one-half of vertebrates studied have disappeared - this is shown as 42% of vertebrate individuals remaining relative to 1970 on the *Planetary Wheel.*[116] This enormous loss of vertebrates may be a good proxy for all life on the planet. We can also extrapolate this recent loss rate into the future. It is all too easy to see that if protection efforts don't improve dramatically, the rest of the wild vertebrates will be gone by 2040. In more detail, of the 177 mammals, for which there is sufficient data to estimate range changes, all 177 mammals have lost 30% of their range relative to 1900. Almost half the mammals have lost more than 80% of their range. For example, the lion's range is now 6% of its historical value.[117]

The evidence for non-mammalian animal declines is just as disturbing. The International Union for Conservation of Nature finds that 42% of terrestrial invertebrates and 35% of marine invertebrates are threatened with extinction.[118] A study in 63 protected areas in Germany, which are presumably somewhat protected from habitat destruction and pesticides, reported a decrease in insect biomass by a whopping 75% over 27 years.[119] Similar crashes have been reported in Puerto Rico and Mexico.[120] The US has experienced losses of commercial honeybees of

[116] World Wildlife Fund. 2016. Living Planet Report 2016. Risk and resilience in a new era. WWF International, Gland, Switzerland

[117] Ceballos, G., P. R. Erhlich and R. Dirzo 2017, "Biological annihilation via the ongoing sixth mass extinction signaled by vertebrate population losses and declines", PNAS E6089-E6096, www.pnas.org/cgi/doi/10.1073/pnas.1704949114

[118] Collen B, Böhm M, Kemp R, Baillie J (2012) Spineless: Status and Trends of the World's Invertebrates (Zoological Soc of London, London).

[119] Hallman, C.A. et al 2017, "More than 75 percent decline over 27 years in total flying insect biomass in protected areas", PLoS One 12 (10) e0185809. https://doi.org/10.1371/journal.pone.0185809

[120] Carrington, D. January 15, 2019 "Insect collapse: We are destroying our life support systems" in The Guardian https://www.theguardian.com/environment/2019/jan/15/insect-collapse-we-are-destroying-our-life-support-systems

40%.[121] The list goes on and on, including extinctions and shrinking ranges of butterflies, birds, amphibians, fish, and pretty much any wild animal which has been studied. A recent study estimated we have lost billions of regional or localized populations of animals.

The decline in numbers of individuals and populations, shrinking ranges and extinction rates has led to the idea that we are entering the sixth mass extinction.[122] It has been called "a frightening assault on the foundations of human civilization".[123] Is this to be our generation's legacy?

## VIII. Healthy soil

You might wonder why I would include soil as one of our critical eight life-sustaining resources. Perhaps you've never given soil much thought. The reason for focusing on soil is because it underpins all land-based life by providing a medium for land plants to grow. Aside from supporting food growth, soil also stores vast quantities of carbon, purifies water, and is a vibrant ecosystem in its own right. The biodiversity in soils is phenomenal. One gram of earth contains a million individual fungi. One quarter of all species on earth are thought to live in the land.[124] If that's not enough to amaze you, did you know that contact with soil increases serotonin and reduces anxiety levels, thus serving as a natural antidepressant?[125] However, we treat the soil like dirt. Fully one-

---

121 https://www.theguardian.com/environment/2019/jun/19/us-beekeepers-lost-40-of-honeybee-colonies-over-past-year-survey-finds accessed July 15, 2019

122 Ceballos, G., P.R. Ehrlich and R. Dirzo 2017, "Biological annihilation via the ongoing sixth mass extinction signaled by vertebrate population losses and declines", Proc. of the Nat. Acad. of Sciences of the USA 114, E6089

123 https://www.huffingtonpost.co.uk/entry/earth-enters-sixth-mass-extinction_n_5964f79fe4b03f144e2e0c0f accessed June 5, 2019

124 European Commission 2010. *The factory of life. Why soil biodiversity is so important*
Luxembourg, ISBN 978-92-79-14998-6 doi 10.2779/17050

125 Wikipedia accessed on November https://en.wikipedia.org/wiki/Mycobacterium_vaccae

third of soil is moderately to highly degraded from the effects of erosion, compaction, salinization, acidification, or chemical pollution.[126] This is shown as 67% of soil remaining, which is not so degraded, in the *Planetary Wheel* figure.

We do not have to go very far back in time to recall the dramatic hardships which soil degradation can cause. In the 1920s, in the midwest of the US, a series of government incentives resulted in a large number of new farms removing native, deep-rooted prairie grasses. A series of not uncommonly dry years followed in the 1930s, causing crops to fail and the soil surface to turn powdery. This powder was subsequently blown around by wind into massive and widespread dust storms. The so-called *Dust Bowl* affected over 100 million acres and blew all the way to the eastern seaboard. Crop failures, loss of topsoil, and financial ruin followed - an estimate $35,000,000 a day were lost in 1936, estimated to be equivalent to $440,000,000 a day in 2017 dollars[127]. There is some evidence that a similar farming-desert link may be responsible for the modern state of the Sahara.[128]

Today, between 25 and 40 billion tonnes of soil are lost to water and wind erosion every year, primarily in agricultural lands where native plants no longer hold the soil in place. This is estimated to be 100 to 1000 times greater than the rate of soil formation. Framing this loss rate in terms of 'the safe operating space' of soil usage, I show the loss of soil as a 0% on the *Planetary Wheel* figure. If current trends continue, we expect to have lost 10% of the global topsoil by the year 2050, or 1.5 million square kilometers of farmland.[129]

---

[126] FAO and ITPS. 2015. Status of the World's Soil Resources (SWSR) – Main Report. Food & Agriculture Organization of the United Nations and Intergovernmental Technical Panel on Soils, Rome, Italy

[127] Wikipedia access October 18, 2018, https://en.wikipedia.org/wiki/Dust_Bowl

[128] Wright, D.K. 2017, *Humans as Agents in the Termination of the African Humid Period,* Frontiers in Earth Science, , DOI=10.3389/feart.2017.00004

[129] FAO and ITPS. 2015. Status of the World's Soil Resources (SWSR) – Main Report. Food & Agriculture Organization of the United Nations and Intergovernmental Technical Panel on Soils, Rome, Italy

In addition to soil loss, intensive farming also imposes large-scale nutrient cycle disruption on soil ecosystems. Vast quantities of nutrients are removed from the soil in the shape of fruit and veg, wood and cotton. Meanwhile, vast quantities of fertilizers are added back. This has led to an upset of soil's natural nitrogen and phosphorus cycles, which are two essential building blocks for plant growth. Gardeners and farmers will recognize these as the N and P of NPK labels on plant food. The planetary boundary study found that these nutrient cycles are already so unbalanced, we are no longer operating within limits that are safe for the survival of humanity. In this case, the safe operating space was defined as the amount of fertilizer that could be added to farmland without leading to oceanic and freshwater dead-zones via eutrophication, as discussed above.[130] I have shown this as 0% in one of soil's slices in the *Planetary Wheel* figure.

With all of soils' assets, its current degraded status, and the multiple pressures it faces, it is no wonder that the UN declared 2016 the *Year of Soils.* We already know how to fix most of these issues without any real hardship. The UN report "Status of the World's Soil Resources" suggests we can reduce soil erosion using cover crops and crop residues, reduce the amount of nitrogen and phosphorus fertilizers used unproductively, and increase their usage in regions of nutrient deficiency. Furthermore, we can improve and share knowledge better.[131] As a consumer, we can financially support farms which practice sustainable methods (see Chapter 4).

---

[130] Steffen, W. et al, 2015, "Planetary boundaries: guiding human development on a changing planet", Science Express Jan 15, 2015, 10.1126/science.1259855

[131] FAO and ITPS 2015. Status of the World's Soil Resources (SWSR) – Main Report. Food & Agriculture Organization of the United Nations and Intergovernmental Technical Panel on Soils, Rome, Italy

# 3 THE DRIVERS OF ENVIRONMENTAL DESTRUCTION

In the previous chapter, we saw that each of the 8 natural resources essential for human life has degraded and that their degradation is ongoing. In this chapter, we explore why that is so. We can look at the causes of eco-depletion from various points of view: from the resources' vantage point, from the consumption angle, or from a who's responsible query. These ways of looking at the issue can, in turn, be phrased as questions: "What drives the loss of wilderness, fresh air, and healthy oceans?", "Which of our activities, food production, transportation, or the healthcare industry, are responsible for the most pollution?", or "Who is driving these losses?". We'll explore these "what, which, and who" approaches below and find that they all focus down to a sharp laser-like answer. Material consumption is laying waste to nature. In particular, the food industry is responsible for a considerable proportion of natural resource loss, contributing over 50% of depletion in many cases. The next largest contributors are transportation and running our homes, which, together with food, account for 70-80% of the loss of many natural resources.

This chapter explores what is driving the reduction of each of the 8 life-sustaining natural resources presented in Chapter 2. While entire books and careers are dedicated to understanding these drivers, here we look at an overview of the significant causes of destruction. I have compiled some of the critical points in Figure 3.1 *The Main Drivers of Natural Resource Depletion*. This approach of laying out all the problems may lead to you feeling overwhelmed and even sad. I don't want you to feel that way. There are easy to remember rules of thumb for changes we can implement that will make a huge difference. This is a winnable battle and surprisingly simple to implement as outlined in the next chapter. I am only including these details so that you'll understand why I claim that we, the people, can solve our environmental problems by changing our consumption patterns.

## What drives the depletion of resources?

### *I. Clean Freshwater*

Three of the main issues affecting clean water and our access to it are dams, water withdrawals, and various kinds of pollution. Roughly half of all river water is moderately to severely affected by dams and if all dams under consideration are built, 93% of water in rivers will not longer flow freely.[132] Dams are useful to humans - providing flood management, water storage, and sometimes electricity. However, such disruption of water flow has dramatic impacts. Ecosystems on both sides of dams are disrupted, including changes to fish migration, sedimentation rates and patterns, and nutrient flows. In addition, 40-80 million people's homes, worldwide, have been displaced by dams.[133]

Globally, agriculture is responsible for 70% water withdrawals, with industry contributing a further 19%.[134] If measured in terms of how much water stress is caused, agriculture drives 93% of water depletion.[135] In the US, the generation of electricity accounts for 41% of withdrawals, slightly larger than agriculture at 40%.[136] The vast majority of agricultural

---

[132] Grill, G. et al 2015, "An index-based framework for assessing patterns and trends in river fragmentation and flow regulation by global dams at multiple scales", Environ. Res. Lett. 10, 015001 doi: 10.1088/1748-9326/10/1/015001

[133] World Commission on Dams Report. Internationalrivers.org. 29 February 2008. Accessed December 16, 2018

[134] http://www.fao.org/aquastat/en/overview/methodology/water-use, accessed January 15, 2020

[135] UN's FAO 2006, "Livestock's long shadow", ISBN 978-92-5-105571-7

[136] https://www.seametrics.com/blog/water-consumers/, accessed Jan 15, 2020

withdrawals are for livestock or their feed crops.[137] To produce a ¼ pound of beef requires 462 gallons (1.74 cubic meters) of water, six times what it takes to produce the same amount of protein in the form of peas and beans.[138] Pork requires 182 gallons, chicken 73, wheat 60, and corn 40 gallons per ¼ pound of food produced.[139]

In addition to removing water from fresh water sources, livestock is probably the largest source of eutrophication, which we explored in Chapter 2, and is when a water ecosystem suffers or dies because of a lack of oxygen in the water. Oxygen deprivation arises when nutrient-rich fertilizer and/or feces runoff into water resulting in an oxygen-gobbling algal bloom. Other water pollutants include pesticide and , antibiotics, dyes, and chemical waste. These are discussed briefly in the toxicant free section below.

## *II. Clean Air*

Outdoor air quality is most affected by coal, tire dust, car emissions, fires (smoke), and dust from degraded lands. Indoor air quality is most affected by heating and cooking fires. In India, the greatest contributor to air pollution deaths is residential biomass burning, resulting in 268,000 deaths a year, followed by coal, (165,000 deaths), and human-induced dust (100,000 deaths). Whereas in China, the biggest contributors to air pollution deaths are coal (283,000 deaths), transportation (137,000), and residential biomass burning (136,000). Globally, there are 7 million annual premature deaths roughly split between indoor and outdoor air pollution. Exposure to indoor or outdoor air pollution increases the risks of asthma, early death from heart and lung disease, and other illnesses[140].

## *III. Toxicant Free Environment*

---

[137] UN's FAO 2006, "Livestock's long shadow", ISBN 978-92-5-105571-7

[138] http://www.project-platforms.com/files/productgallery-new.php accessed December 11, 2018

[139] https://www.seametrics.com/blog/water-consumers/, accessed January 15, 2020

[140] State of Global Air 2018, Health Effects Institute, Special Report, Boston, Ma

It is challenging to itemize the worst sources of toxic pollutants as there are so many kinds of toxicants and so many kinds of impacts. Pure Earth, a not for profit organization founded to solve pollution problems, has ranked the industries which cause the highest loss of healthy years of life. They estimate that 7-17 million years are lost annually to toxic pollution. Lead-acid battery recycling tops the Pure Earth list followed by mining and ore processing, tanneries, dumpsites, industrial estates, smelting, artisanal small-scale gold mining, product manufacturing, chemical manufacturing, and the dye industry.[141]

In another summary, The World Health Organization lists the chemicals which are of significant public health concern, in decreasing order: air pollution, arsenic, asbestos, benzene, cadmium, dioxins, inadequate or excess fluoride, lead, mercury, and pesticides.[142] Whereas, The Stockholm Convention of Persistent Organic Chemicals identifies 9 of the 12 deadliest pollutants as pesticides.[143] Pesticides are partially responsible for bee colony-collapse-disorder in which beehive numbers have crashed, as well as in the dramatic decline of insect numbers globally.[144] Fifty percent of pesticide use in the US is for livestock and their feed.[145]

## *IV. Healthy Soils*

The loss of healthy soil is, of course, overwhelmingly dominated by the food industry. Our top soils are so degraded that experts warn that further damage will severely impact food security[146]. Livestock and its feed are the main drivers in the loss of healthy soils.[147]

---

[141] Pure Earth and Green Cross 2016, The World's Worst Pollution Problems: The Toxins beneath our Feet"

[142] WHO 2010 "Preventing disease through Healthy Environments"

[143] Stockholm Convention on Persistent Organic Pollutants

[144] Sánchez-Bayo, F. & K.A.G. Wyckhuys 2019 "Worldwide decline of the entomofauna: A review of its drivers", Biological Conservation 232, 8

[145] UN's FAO 2006, "Livestock's long shadow", ISBN 978-92-5-105571-7

[146] FAO of the UN 2015 "Status of the World's Soil Resources"

[147] UN's FAO 2006, "Livestock's long shadow", ISBN 978-92-5-105571-7

## *V. Healthy Oceans*

The UN's First Global Integrated Marine Assessment, published in 2016, lists several areas of concern, including:

- The rate at which we remove fish and other resources from the ocean is far faster than the speed of regeneration. This imbalance has resulted in depleted fish stocks and unsettled ecosystems. One result of over harvesting is the smothering of coral reefs by algae, arising because the numbers of fish who used to eat the algae are greatly reduced[148]. Twenty-four percent of harvested fish are used as livestock feed.[149]
- Detrimental encroachment of human activities on the ocean includes fishing, shipping lanes, mining, and wind farms.
- Pollution from industry, agriculture, sewage, and plastics negatively impacts the oceans. Livestock drives a large proportion of nutrient dumping, contributing to a recent ten-fold increase in dead zones in the seas.[150] Most litter in the seas is from food packaging, which makes its way from all parts of the world into the ocean via rivers.
- Climate change affects sea level rise, ocean acidification, and changes to ocean currents with ramifications for the mixing of ocean water, oxygen levels, and weather patterns.

The UN report concludes that the best way forward is to develop a coherent strategy to address all these issues together. We now have scattered laws addressing specific problems, but we need to move towards a comprehensive ocean protection strategy that takes into account interacting pressures. The report further argues that there are known solutions, but they aren't always implemented. As consumers, we can buy Marine Stewardship Council certified fish and support initiatives aimed at protecting the oceans.[151]

---

[148] UN 2016, The First Global Integrated Marine Assessment, http://www.worldoceanassessment.org/

[149] UN's FAO 2006, "Livestock's long shadow", ISBN978-92-5-105571-7

[150] Deadzone increase by factor of 10

[151] UN 2016, The First Global Integrated Marine Assessment, http://www.worldoceanassessment.org/

## *VI. Wildlands*

Food production dominates our loss of wildlands. Thirty percent of all non-ice and non-barren rock land on the planet is dedicated to the raising of meat.[152] Seventy percent of previously forested Amazonia is now pasture and feedstock covers most of the rest of the deforested area. Global analyses of land use show over and over again that conversion of wilderness to crops and pasture drives the vast majority of the loss of terrestrial wilderness. While built-up areas and roads cover only 1-2% of land, they have a disproportionately large impact on reducing wilderness by creating barriers and fragmenting ecosystems, as well as by facilitating further encroachment on the wilderness.[153]

## *VII. Biodiversity*

The loss and fragmentation of wildlands is the leading cause of the loss of biodiversity, particularly when we focus on the decrease in the numbers of wild plants and animals. For example, in the World Wildlife Fund's ongoing study of vertebrates, roughly 50% of threats to 703 terrestrial populations were habitat loss and degradation. The remainder of the threats come from overexploitation (25%), invasive species (11%), pollution (7%), and climate change (7%). As noted above, the loss of habitat is overwhelmingly dominated by agriculture, especially meat and dairy[154]. Many other studies reinforce these findings.[155, 156, 157]

---

[152] UN's FAO 2006, "Livestock's long shadow", ISBN 978-92-5-105571-7

[153] ten Brink, B. 2010, Netherlands Environmental Assessment Agency, *Rethinking Global Biodiversity Strategies*

[154] World Wildlife Fund 2016, "The Living Planet Report"

[155] Diaz, S. et al 2019, Draft of "Summary for policymakers of the global assessment report on biodiversity & ecosystem services of the Intergovernmental Science-Policy Platform on Biodiversity& Ecosystem Services"

[156] Ceballos, G., P.R. Ehrlich & R. Dirzo 2017, Proc. Nat. Acad. of Sciences of the USA 114, E6089

[157]ten Brink, B. 2010, Netherlands Environmental Assessment Agency, *Rethinking Global Biodiversity Strategies*

## *VIII. Stable Climate*

According to the US Environmental Protection Agency, the largest human contributions to greenhouse gases in the atmosphere are: electricity and heat production (25%), Agriculture, Forestry and Other Land Use (24%), Industry (21%) and transportation (14%) and buildings and other energy making up the last 16%[158]. A sizeable chunk of greenhouse gas emissions, 18%, is due to livestock.[159] So while it is great to see efforts to improve our gas mileage and concern about air travel -- these are not the only emissions we need to address.[160]

In summary, the conversion of wilderness to fields and pastures, primarily for livestock, is the cause of the loss of the majority of wilderness, biodiversity, and soils. Agriculture also dominates water withdrawals and is perhaps the greatest contributor to both fresh and oceanic water quality degradation. In the oceans, the drive for fish, for both human and livestock consumption, is destroying ocean ecosystems. So our appetite for meat and fish is the main cause of the loss of wilderness, biodiversity, soils, clean water and healthy oceans, 5 of our 8 essential life sustaining resources. While not necessarily the main culprit leading losses to our other three resources, livestock still has a significant impact on them. Livestock is responsible for about 18% greenhouse gas emissions, and pesticides used in agriculture make up three-quarters of the 12 deadliest pollutants. Only fresh air is not directly degraded by livestock production on a global scale. For further reading, the UN report *Livestock's Long Shadow* is an excellent introduction, even if slightly dated.[161]

---

[158] https://www.epa.gov/ghgemissions/global-greenhouse-gas-emissions-data#Reference%201 accessed December 16, 2018

[159] UN's FAO 2006, "Livestock's long shadow", ISBN 978-92-5-105571-7

[160] McKie, Aug 3, 2019 "We must change food production to save the world...", The Guardian, https://www.theguardian.com/environment/2019/aug/03/ipcc-land-use-food-production-key-to-climate-crisis-leaked-report

[161] UN's FAO 2006, "Livestock's long shadow", ISBN 978-92-5-105571-7

## Figure 3.1 The Main Drivers of Natural Resource Depletion

| Natural Resources | Main Drivers of their depletion |
|---|---|
| Fresh water | Agriculture is responsible for 93% of water depletion, dominated by water withdrawals to support livestock. Raising livestock also drives most of water pollution,[A] including 78% of eutrophication.[B] |
| Clean air | Burning fuel for cooking and heating dominates indoor air pollution. Transport, coal, & industry are the major sources of outdoor air pollution.[C] |
| Toxicant free | The world's worst pollution problems include battery manufacture and disposal, mining; tanneries, dyeing and other industrial sources.[D] Raising livestock leads to the use of 9 of the world's 12 deadliest pollutants.[E] In the US, livestock is responsible for 37% of pesticide use.[A] |
| Healthy soil | In the USA, livestock drives 55% of soil erosion and 1/3 of the loss of the soil nutrients nitrogen and phosphorous.[A] |
| Healthy oceans | Plastic pollution is mostly from food packaging and plastic decay. Ocean acidification, and rising temperatures and sea level, are primarily driven by rising carbon dioxide. The depletion of fish stocks is driven by overfishing, with a notable 24% of fish captures used to feed livestock.[F] |
| Wild lands | Livestock uses 30% of the global land surface, accounting for most of the loss of wilderness. Livestock rearing directly drives at least 70% of Amazonian deforestation, and, arguably more than 90% as farming roads open up areas for development.[A] |
| Biodiversity | Habitat loss is the main hazard to 85% of threatened birds, amphibians and mammals, which in turn is driven by grazing of livestock and growing feed crops for livestock.[A] |
| Stable climate | The loss of a stable climate is driven by mankind's emissions of greenhouse gas. In terms of $CO_2$ equivalents, industry is responsible for 33% of our emissions, buildings for 18%, transportation for 14%,[G] and livestock for 18%[A] |

**A.** Livestock's Long Shadow 2006, FAO Rome **B.** Poore, J. & T. Nemecek 2018 "Reducing food's environmental impacts through producers and consumers", Science 360 (6392) 987. **C.** State of Global Air 2018. Special Report. Boston, MA:Health Effects Institute. **D.** Pure Earth and Green Cross 2016, The World's Worst Pollution Problems: The Toxins beneath our Feet" **E.** Stockholm Convention of Persistent Organic Pollutants 2016 **F.** The State of World Fisheries and Aquaculture 2008, FAO of the UN Rome 2009. **G.** IPCC 2014 Climate Change 2014 Synthesis Report.

## Which of our activities drive the most environmental destruction?

The conclusion of the previous section, that the livestock industry is responsible for the majority of environmental depletion, is soundly affirmed by many studies. In this section, we'll explore some of these confirming studies through the lens of assessing the environmental impact of various categories of consumption. The consumption categories are things like food, transport, and clothing. One of the most common methods to assess the impact of consumption on the environment is to reduce the impacts to a common currency like money, as in economic models, or to land area used, as in eco-footprint analyses. These common currency approaches are useful for understanding the relative share of resource use. We'll discuss them below. But the artificialness of reducing everything to a dollar or an acre bothers my physicist brain that wants to keep apples with apples and not with oranges. I'm therefore drawn to the studies which assess the impact of consumption on a suite of natural resources.

Tucker et al. (2006) is an excellent example of such a "suite study." They looked at the net impact of various consumption categories on eight resources. Five of their resources are the same as those considered in Chapter 2 of this book, including fresh air, fresh water, clean oceans, a toxicant free environment, and a stable climate. Tucker et al. did not include wilderness, biodiversity, or healthy soils but instead included the loss of the nonrenewable resources oil, coal, and metals as their three other natural resources. They found that the depletion of all eight of these resources were driven by, from highest to least: 1. food and drink, 2. transport, 3. housing including furniture, equipment, and utility use, 4. clothing, 5. healthcare, 6. communication, 7. recreation, 8. education, 9. restaurants and hotels, and 10. miscellaneous. The first three, food, transport, and housing, accounted for 70-80% of the loss of eight resources.[162] The three natural resources Tucker et al. didn't include, which I

[162] Tucker, A. Et al 2006, "Environmental Impact of Products (EIPRO): Analysis of the life cycle environmental impacts related to the final consumption of the EU-25", European Commission JRC EUR 22285 EN

**70-80% of natural resource depletion is caused by just 3 consumption categories:**

**Food**
**Transport**
**Running our homes**

did, are the three I found impacted the most by food - biodiversity, wilderness, and soil.

These conclusions are powerful because they give us a way to prioritize the most effective things we can do, and these are primarily connected to activities at home or to and from home. Consumption categories outside of the home play their role, of course. But if we can green our domestic consumption, including to and from home, we can reduce 70-80% of natural resource depletion. I find that hugely empowering.

A study by the European Environment Agency found similar results. Together, food, construction, agriculture and fishing, electricity and gas, and water were responsible for 58% of material input, 37% of ozone precursors, 52% of acidifying emissions, and 42% of greenhouse gases. So quite a different list of impacts but a similar conclusion. They also found that the highest environmental impact, per Euro spent, was in household goods and services. Such a high impact per money spent means that household changes would yield the largest positive impact per Euro.[163]

## The impact of food on the environment

Taking this multi-resource-impact analysis further, Poore and Nemecek (2017) focused on the impact of food on a set of five natural resources. They compiled the results of 570 studies representing over 38,000 farms and the production of 90% of global protein and calorie consumption. They found that the full life cycle of food accounts for 26% of greenhouse gas emissions.

---

163 EEA Technical report No 2. “Environmental pressures from European Consumption and production: A study in integrated environmental and economic analysis”

**Table 3.1 Resources to produce 100 grams of protein**

| | GHG (kg $CO_2$) | Land Use ($m^2$) | Acid (g $SO_2$) | Eutro-phication (g P) | Water Scarcity (kiloliters) |
|---|---|---|---|---|---|
| Beef | 50 | 162 | 90 | 105 | 20 |
| Cheese | 11 | 41 | 75 | 35 | 50 |
| Pork | 7.6 | 11 | 80 | 75 | 40 |
| Farmed fish | 6.0 | 3.7 | 90 | 75 | 50 |
| Chicken | 5.7 | 7.1 | 60 | 20 | 10 |
| Eggs | 4.2 | 5.7 | 35 | 20 | 20 |
| Peas | 2.0 | 2.2 | 5 | 5 | 8 |
| Nuts | 0.3 | 7.9 | 20 | 10 | 50 |
| Grains | 2.7 | 4.6 | 10 | 20 | 30 |

Measures are 1. GHG - greenhouse gas emissions, in units of kilograms of carbon dioxide equivalents, 2. Land used in meters squared, which is about 1.2 square yards, 3. Acid - terrestrial acidification, in terms of grams of sulfur dioxide emitted, $SO_2$, 4. Eutrophication in the units of grams of phosphate, and 5. Water scarcity in kiloliters (264 gallons). From Poore and Nemecek 2018

32% of terrestrial acidification, 78% of eutrophication, covers 43% of the world's ice and desert free land, and drives 90-95% of water use when weighted by water-scarcity. Water-scarcity weights water withdrawals by how much impact the withdrawals have on water stress.[164] Together, these food impacts have astoundingly large and broad implications on natural resource depletion.

Poore and Nemecek dug deeper and explored the impact of producing 100 grams of protein for various kinds of food, reproduced here in Table 3.1 *Resources to produce 100 grams of protein*. They found huge variability in the ranges of resources used for a given food type, which highlights that the version of a given food we buy can have a significant effect. But by looking at the average impacts of the various food types, we can understand relative impact of different types of food. Unsurprisingly, meat has a far greater impact than grains and vegetables, pound for pound. This is because a cow has to eat and drink throughout her lifetime. The higher resource needs of meat is in line with biology's rule of thumb that for each step up the food chain, e.g. from plants to herbivores, the energy required to support life at the higher level increases by a factor of 10. This factor of 10 coincides with an urban legend that has floated around for years, which is that vegetable protein takes about 1/10th the land that animal protein requires. This is not a hard and fast rule, but a useful rule of thumb nonetheless. Cheese lies somewhere between meat and veg -- as it is a product of an animal but isn't a single-use product like meat. A female mammal, of course, can produce lots of milk over her lifetime rather than one set amount of steak, hamburger, and so forth.

It is also important to remember that just because a product uses less land or other resources to produce it, doesn't necessarily make it an ethical choice. Consider, for example, battery chickens who live their lives in cages which are so small they can't flap their wings, let alone walk, they have their beaks trimmed to eliminate pecking, and they experience high rates of

---

[164] Poore, J. & T. Nemecek 2018 "Reducing food's environmental impacts through producers and consumers", Science 360 (6392) 987-992, 01 Jun 2018, doi: 10.1126/science.aaq0216

osteoporosis leading to rates of knee breakages up to 24%.[165] So while battery cage rearing uses very little land, keeping an animal in this way is morally problematic.

In addition to animal welfare ethics, there are human health and social justice reasons for avoiding factory-farmed meats. Health-wise, intensively reared chickens have more calories from fat than protein and ⅙ of the omega-3 fatty acid relative to the chickens in the 1970s. Omega-3 reduces the risk of heart attack, stroke, type II diabetes, and depression, as well as improving metabolic functions and promoting healthy child development. Intensively reared chicken is not a healthy option -- beware of inexpensive chicken at the grocery store and fast-food chicken. Likewise, farmed salmon has ½ the Omega-3 fatty acids relative to wild salmon, with a similar reduction for tilapia and carp.[166]

Some folk may worry about the health implications of reducing our meat intake. According to the well-respected Mayo Clinic, it is easy to meet our nutritional needs with a vegetarian diet given a little planning - as is also necessary for a healthy omnivorous diet. The Clinic further points out that a diet with less meat reduces the risk of heart disease, diabetes, and some cancers.[167] A fully vegetarian world is estimated to reduce global mortality by 10% and benefit society to the tune of 10% of gross domestic product.[168]

But aside from going fully vegetarian, many of us could reduce our meat intake with positive health and budget outcomes. The USDA estimates that nearly 60% of Americans eat more than the recommended daily allowance of protein. The recommended daily allowance of protein is 0.66 grams per kilogram of body weight, so for a 150 pound (66 kg) person, this means 0.1 pounds

---

165 https://en.wikipedia.org/wiki/Battery_cage accessed August 14, 2019

166 World Wildlife Fund 2017, Appetite for Destruction

167https://www.mayoclinic.org/healthy-lifestyle/nutrition-and-healthy-eating/in-depth/vegetarian-diet/art-20046446

168 Nuwer, R. 2016, “What would happen if the world suddenly went vegetarian?”, BBC, https://www.bbc.com/future/article/20160926-what-would-happen-if-the-world-suddenly-went-vegetarian

(45 grams) of protein a day.[169] A study, which excluded the impacts of cooking and waste, found that shifting from an average American's diet to the recommended diet reduced food related carbon emissions by 25%, eutrophication contributions by 21% and land use by 18%.[170] If we cut waste, which accounts for at least a third of food production, those savings would more than double. The World Wildlife Fund has estimated that if we all followed recommended daily diets, 13% of agricultural land would be freed up.[171] That's a lot of land!

And if we went whole hog and got all our protein from non-meat sources, we'd free up more than 6 billion acres for wilderness.[172] This represents 18% of the global land surface, with its inherent services of supporting biodiversity, cleaning water, producing fresh air, and carbon sequestration. This is a dramatic chunk of the suggested ½ for nature. What's more, a no-animal-product food supply would reduce global greenhouse gas emissions by a whooping 28%.[173] If the world became vegan, there would of course be lots and lots to work out. For instance, how would we protect historically pastoral lands which have their own unique ecosystems and how would we help livestock farmers transition to other jobs?

Moving on from how-what-we-eat-impacts-the-environment to the impacts of the companies from which we buy our food. The

---

[169]https://health.gov/dietaryguidelines/2015/guidelines/chapter-2/current-eating-patterns-in-the-united-states/

[170] Behrens, P. et al 2017, "Evaluating the environmental impacts of dietary recommendations", PNAS 114, 13412

[171] World Wildlife Fund 2017, Appetite for Destruction

[172] This calculation is based on the fact that currently 8 billion acres, representing 25% of the global land surface, is currently used for meat production (UNCCD 2017, UN Global Land Outlook). And the assumption that converting 20% of the current meat producing land, or 1.6 billion acres, would be sufficient to replace the food we get from meat. Based on estimates discussed above this is probably twice as much land as would be needed to replace livestock in our diets. Using this conservative estimate, 80% of land currently used to produce meat, or 6.4 billion acres, would be freed from agriculture.

[173] Poore, J. & T. Nemecek, 2019, Erratum for the Research Article "Reducing food's environmental impacts through producers and consumers", *Science* 363, eaaw9908

2013 Oxfam report, Behind the Brands, delves identifies 10 companies that basically control the global food industry. Each of the 10 companies have revenues higher than lower-income countries, and they exert inordinate political power. In addition, they control the working conditions of millions of people and are able to, and often do, ignore environmental concerns.

Although the Big 10 are making efforts to be more environmentally and socially conscious, in large part because consumers are demanding better, they are still primarily about profit. There have been recent instances of controversial land acquisitions and unacceptable working conditions, including inadequate sanitation and unprotected use of pesticides, underage workers, underpayment, denial of long-term contracts, and causing water poverty for people living near Big 10 farms. Furthermore, small scale farmers have difficulty competing with the Big 10, and their market shares have inevitably shrunk, which is a travesty. Not only has this destroyed family businesses, but local farmers are the folk who know the land and often act as stewards of knowledge and biodiversity.[174]

After food production, transport and running our homes have the next most significant impacts on our natural resources. For two of our eight resources, we know the percentage contribution of different sectors. But beyond these, I could not find breakdowns of the impacts of consumption categories, including for running our homes and transport. For climate change, we know that home energy use contributes 31% of greenhouse gas emissions, followed by industrial energy use at 21% and transport at 14%.[175] We also know the percentages of global land use. On the broadest scale, 37% of all land is given over to agriculture, 31% is still forested, 2-3% is built up, and the remainder is ice-covered, rocky, or supports other ecosystems.[176] Of that land which is farmed, 80% of it is used for livestock either as pasture

---

[174] Oxfam 2013, Behind the Brands, Oxfam Briefing Paper 166

[175] The Intergovernmental Panel on Climate Change 2014- The synthesis report of the 5 Assessment Report. https://www.ipcc.ch/report/ar5/syr/

[176] http://databank.worldbank.org/data/home.aspx accessed December 12, 2018

land or through growing feed crops[177]. But beyond those two resource categories, I could not find compressive estimates of the percentage contributions of various activities to resource depletion.

## Who can best reduce resource depletion?

Besides exploring which consumption categories drive the degradation of our natural resources, we can also examine which actors are ultimately responsible for resource depletion. Is it the big industrial farming companies and other large scale businesses? Is it our governments? Is it individuals? Perhaps a more effective question to ask is "Who can change society's consumption patterns?" Is it big business, governments, the wealthy, individuals?

We could attribute natural resource depletions to industry and manufacturing, governments, or a greedy wealthy class. And certainly, these big actors do play a role. However, I subscribe to an alternative perspective. I believe that the impact of industry and governments are symptoms, not the underlying cause, of resource depletion. These large-scale players are followers not social leaders. They are capitalizing on cultural trends. Businesses produce products we'll buy and governments are in power because they have promised to work on issues important to their voters. There are, of course, many cases of misleading and downright false advertising and campaigning. And we desperately need to stop those responsible for such deceptions. But the fundamental principle holds that products are made because people will buy them, and leaders are elected who are meant to represent the will of the populace. And of course, we wouldn't want it any other way - no one wants a leader or a producer who imposes their ideology on us.

Further, whether we lay the blame of eco-depletion directly on the shoulders of industry and government or view big-actors as responding to the public will, business and government will only act to protect the environment if we show that we care about the

---

[177] UN's FAO 2006, "Livestock's long shadow", ISBN 978-92-5-105571-7

natural world. And the most effective way we can show we care is with our cash and our votes. If CEOs change production strategies to protect the environment, which may well cost more money in the short-term, their shareholders may fire them, and many consumers may stop buying their products if prices rise. In a way, the CEO is stuck until we change our collective spending patterns. And likewise for politicians. They can't enact environmental protection laws without our support.

Our consumer choices are, of course, imposed upon by large scale organizations. But we are independent. For instance we can survive a boycott of a given product and even bankruptcy. But none of the big actors can remain in their roles without our support. And they are all empowered by the same thing: cash flows. Manufacturers who produce less expensive products will out-compete other producers in a standard bottom-line-is-all world. Candidates who outspend other campaigners are more likely to gain office, and once in office are often influenced by those who funded them. The ultra-wealthy gained their status through capitalist ventures, of course. As deflating as money-underlies-everything might feel, it gives us a powerful lever. If we change how we spend our money, we *will* change how the world works. This brings us to economics.

## How the standard economic model fails to protect the environment

One way to explore what drives environmental depletion is the approach of the standard economic model. In this model, consumption and the rate of resource use are considered as primarily driven by 3 factors: population numbers, affluence, and technology (see Figure 3.2 *The Standard Economic Model and Possible Fixes*). The theory goes that as population and affluence grow, consumption and resource use increase, countered by technological improvements. In the past, many proponents of the standard economic model took it as a given that smarter design would offset expansions in population and affluence, and thus resource use would level out.

However, comprehensive research on resource use has shown that rising consumption outpaces improvements in efficiency such that resource use continues to increase[178]. A familiar example is fuel consumption. While miles per gallon have increased by 30% for cars, since 1980, and 40% for airplanes, since 1975, overall consumption in both has increased because there is more travel. Similarly, the efficiency of refrigerators and air conditions increased by 10% and 17% respectively since 1980, but in the same time, the number of units increased by 20% and 30%.[179] Increased consumption arising from increased efficiency is sometimes referred to as the rebound effect and it is very common. So while technological advances are wonderful, when embedded in current consumption patterns, they are not a magic wand to solve our environmental ills. To confirm this, we have only to look at the fact that the last 50 years of rapid technological advances have been accompanied by an *acceleration* of the destruction of the natural world, not a decrease.[180]

The standard economic model explains this acceleration of consumption as the result of the concurrent growth in population and affluence. The last few decades have seen tremendous international efforts to curtail population growth, resulting in a slow down of the rate but still an increase of slightly over than 1% per year.[181] Affluence is also continuing to rise. For instance, the eco-footprint of the average American grew by 181% between 1971 and 2005.[182] So while growth has previously been viewed as a good, especially in mainstream economics, many are recognizing that unbridled growth is causing drastic reductions of our natural resources. The rise in the numbers of consumers and their

---

[178] EEA Technical report No 2. "Environmental pressures from European Consumption and production: A study in integrated environmental and economic analysis"

[179] Schor, J.B. 2010 True Wealth, Penguin Books, page 90

[180] Diaz, S. et al 2019 "Summary for policymakers of the global assessment report on biodiversity & ecosystem services of the Intergovernmental Science-Policy Platform on biodiversity & ecosystem services"

[181] https://data.worldbank.org/indicator/sp.pop.grow accessed August 1, 2019

[182] Global Footprint Network, https://www.footprintnetwork.org

affluence are both unsustainable. Together, they are causing havoc. Frighteningly, even if population and affluence leveled out, we'd still be depleting our natural resources at a rate faster than they are replenished. What's more, it costs us more to not protect our resources, than it would cost to take care of them.

For these and other reasons, economists are now questioning the assumptions underlying the standard model. In particular, there is a growing recognition of the danger in not accounting for the use of common resources for which manufacturers do not have to pay. These free goods and services are external to the standard model and are thus called externalities. Depletion is the end result when individuals can use common goods for their own benefit without having to consider the impacts. This depletion is called the 'tragedy of the commons.'

The recognition of the tragedy of the commons has led to the suggestion of full economic costing. In such an economy, a product's cost would include the cost to protect and repair the environment and human health for all stages of the product's life from manufacturing, through use, and the disposal of, the item. While I applaud the principles behind full economic costing, I'm not a big fan. First of all, it will take too long to implement full economic costing to prevent the imminent environmental disasters. Can you imagine the bickering that would ensue? Second, how do we put a price on a prairie or a life? Should we even be considering such a valuation?

Another set of externalities to the standard economic models are injustices. Standard economics leads to injustices today, such as people living near resources or factories suffering for the sake of consumption by others. Driven by bottom-line economics, poor resource management leads to water scarcity, polluted air, toxic pollutants, climate instability, soil losses, and loss of local wilderness, as well as poor health. And the poorer one is, the more these damages hurt, for you have fewer options to reduce their impact. The tragedy of the commons also drives intergenerational injustice. Future generations will suffer because of our actions today. Intergenerational and current-day injustices are thus added to the weighty reasons of loss of ecosystems and their services as to why we must alter how we consume.

***Figure 3.2 The Standard Economic Model and Possible Fixes***

**STANDARD ECONOMIC MODEL**

**DRIVERS**

**POPULATION**: Following tremendous efforts to curtail growth, still rising by 1.2% / year

**AFFLUENCE:** Average per capita spending in the US has doubled since 1970

**TECHNOLOGY**: Reduce environmental impact of products

***ENVIRONMENTAL IMPACTS*** *rise with population and affluence, but decrease with technological advances*

**OLD CONCLUSIONS**
Technological advances can counter rises in population and affluence

**NEW CONCLUSIONS**
Even mainstream economists now say we must stop focus on growth or grow very differently.

**External to and neglected by the standard model**

LOSS OF NATURAL CAPITAL: air, water, forests, soils, oceans, biodiversity

DEGRADATION OF ECOSYSTEM SERVICES: climate regulation, waste processing, purifying air and water

INJUSTICE: rich/poor, future generations, other species

**POSSIBLE FIXES**

| | |
|---|---|
| **Techno fixes** | Good, but … not keeping up with population and affluence growth. |
| **Policy, laws and treaties** | Good, but … many moderate successes but neither comprehensive nor stemming ongoing destruction. Slow. |
| **Ecological costing** | Flawed? Complex to implement. 'Pricing-life' objections. No current working example. |
| **Market will right itself** | Flawed. Does not account for natural or social capital. Economists increasingly rejecting market solution. |

**Personal Action**

Win / win / win
good for wallet, health, justice, resilient ecosystems, plants, animals, climate, and the community

We can do it RIGHT NOW

Drives market, policy, techno, and eco-costing fixes

Responsible and rational

*Data from* True Wealth*, Schor 2011 and* https://www.statista.com/statistics/247455/annual-us-consumer-expenditures/

# The two-edged sword of personal responsibility.

None of the following have been successful at protecting the environment: government, policies, big business, industry, market forces, nor technology. There are ecological laws, treaties, tax incentives, watchdog groups, petitions, and great scientific advances. These efforts are slowing depletion, but the destruction of the natural world is outpacing its regenerative abilities. We know this because we continue to lose soil, air, water, and ecosystems which make our lives possible. The only thing which can stop this destruction is us. How we spend and invest our money, and how we vote are our best tools. Our spending and voting patterns influence what is produced and how it is produced. How we spend our money sends political, social, and cultural signals to our lawmakers, our judiciary, our policy makers, manufacturers, our neighbors, our families, and our colleagues.

The acknowledgment that individual consumer spending is the critical lever that is capable of adequately reducing natural resource depletion is a sharp two-sided coin. On the one hand, 'Power to the People' is right here (Yipee!), and we can stop our support of destructive practices straight away. But on the other hand, putting the onus on the individual is not a very appealing message. Neither manufacturers nor politicians, not even non-profits, want to be the ones to say "Stop buying so much stuff". I think this is the main reason we don't hear the message that it is individuals' consumer patterns that are driving the destruction of the natural world. Asking or telling an individual to stick to any given moral stance doesn't go over well in the best of times.

However, and this is critical, eco-conscious choices are actually of huge benefit to the individual and to society. Green lifestyles improve physical and mental health, and increase wealth equity, intergenerational justice, and democracy. I believe that only love can solve the modern tangle of problems we face. Protecting nature, or if you prefer, creation is the ultimate act of love and respect for other beings -- human and otherwise. But I get ahead of myself as this is the topic of the following chapter, so let's return to our discussion of the drivers of environmental destruction.

## Eco-footprints

Another way to measure one's impacts on nature are eco-footprints. These are estimates of the *amount of land* that would be needed to support one's lifestyle - including all the resources we consume, such as food and mobile phones, as well as how much land is required to absorb and clean our waste. For eco-footprints, land is the common currency onto which all other impacts are mapped. This is a very clever idea, and has its uses. It is excellent for communication and discussions about equal rights across continents, as well as across economic scales and time. But I do feel it distorts the relative importance of various activities. While it is scientifically valid that land absorbs carbon, looking at the problem in this way suggests that carbon emissions are by far the biggest challenge we face. I don't argue with the tenet that carbon emission reduction is vital, but it is only one of many issues. I worry that focusing on eco-footprints, or any other single metric for that matter, can get us into trouble. For example, by focusing on land-area-use of a product, one could arrive at the conclusion that 'Battery chickens are good'. Similarly, the modern habit of focusing on the price of products has led to the current tragedy of environmental destruction and social injustices.

My reservations about eco-footprints aside, they are thought-provoking and provide an elegant summary. And I like that their currency is land, rather than dollars. So here we go. In Table 3.2 *Some Eco-footprints,* I've listed some footprint calculations from the Global Footprint network. I used their calculator, at https://www.footprintcalculator.org, and found that my footprint is 3.1 global hectares. That's about 36% of the footprint of the average American and I don't find it a chore to have this relatively low footprint. However, if everyone on earth were to have a lifestyle like me, we'd need 1.9 Earths to support us. If every human were to have a 'fair share' of earth's resources, our footprint should be one Earth or less. So, how could I halve mine?

| Table 3.2 Some Eco-Footprints | | |
|---|---|---|
| One person | Eco-footprint<br>Land need to provide and regenerate resources one person | Earths needed<br>How many earths needed if everyone lived like this person |
| Average person globally | 2.8 global hectares | 1.7 Earths |
| Average American | 8.4 global hectares | 5.1 Earths |
| Average Brit | 4.8 global hectares | 2.9 Earths |
| The author | 3.1 global hectares | 1.9 Earths |
| Fair share | 1.6 global hectares | 1 Earth |
| Comments | A global hectare is roughly 100 meters squared making it 2.5 acres. It is slightly different from a standard hectare as it takes into account the productivity of the land. | When this column exceeds one, we are using resources at a rate faster than the Earth regenerates them, and are thus eating into our natural capital |

Like the average global person, almost half of my footprint is for land to absorb carbon from the roughly 10 miles I drive every day (0.3 global hectares), the annual cross Atlantic flight to visit family (0.8 global hectares), and food transportation (0.3 global hectares). My footprint is less than other American's primarily because I'm (mostly) a vegetarian, which reduces my footprint by 3.4 global hectares. My eco-footprint is further reduced by using renewable energy to heat our home, signing up for renewable electricity, conserving energy where I can, and eating local in-season foods as much as I can. How can I get in line with a fair share? I could get halfway there by giving up seeing my family across the Atlantic every year. That's difficult. But something to consider. My eco-footprint tells a similar story to both the resource-focused and the consumption category discussions above. All three conclude that my food has the most significant environmental impact, followed by home heating and electricity usage, and transportation.

## Material extraction

As a final way of looking at what drives natural resource depletion, we can look at how much stuff is dug up from the earth to support our lifestyle. Can you guess, over what timeframe 162 pounds / 73.5 kg of material are extracted from the Earth for each US resident? I may have guessed that this was over a year, but I'd have been way off. 162 pounds of earth are extracted every day to support each American's life.[183] The global average is 60 pounds a day. Doesn't that seem like an outrageous amount of the earth being dug up every day? Oftentimes its even for products we're not that interested in or use only once. Global extraction rates tripled between 1970 and 2010, during which time the population has roughly doubled. We are extracting more per capita as we become more technologically developed. None of us are setting out to harm nature deliberately, but the way we spend our money is funding this extraction and its consequent destruction of nature.

After years of cycling through doing environmental research, and engaging with community activism and campaigning, I have settled on personal spending is the key lever for change. Not that campaigning, letter writing, contributing to

[183] Schanel, H. et al 2016, Global Material Flows and Resource Productivity, Assessment Report for the UNEP International Resource Panel, ISBN: 978-92-807-3554-3

policy discussions, research and so forth aren't important, not at all. But for wide scale change, how we spend our money is the lifeblood of our economy and our greatest influencer. My research for this book has solidified this stance. Of course, there are other important fronts on which to address the enormous environmental challenges we face, but for me, as a minimum, I need my own house to be in order. I need my drop of impact to be positive. I hope that you can see that this point of view is, at least, self-consistent and striving to be morally sound. Incidentally, this is how I feel about my evangelical relatives' point of view. I respect them for their commitment, their open-mindedness, and their kindness. No matter who you are, I hope that you can understand why so many of us want to change our consumption patterns and even contribute to these efforts more widely. Just how we can go about this is the subject of the next chapter.

# 4 WHAT CAN WE DO?
## CONSUME FEWER MATERIAL GOODS

Material consumption underpins the extraction of matter from the earth, as well as the garbage and pollution we put back into nature. A critical way we can influence what is extracted and returned is, of course, to change how we purchase. We can start with buying less: less meat, less plastic, less electronics, and less fossil fuels. Next, we can throw away less by repairing, borrowing, donating, and repurposing. When we buy things, we can choose long-term and multi-purpose products. These reductions may sound like a horrendous list of impositions and guilt trips to you. I get that. On the other hand, I'm frustrated by the talk of these sorts of choices being a sacrifice. So, before we get into a discussion of how to improve our environmental impacts, let me take a moment to outline some of the benefits these choices afford us.

Wise eco-choices result in better physical and mental health, greater resilience, diversification of wealth, and strengthened social networks. Beyond personal rewards, eco-conscious consumption can act to reduce wealth inequality and intergenerational injustices, and to strengthen democracy. Eco-conscious living can also help to solve many of our modern-day social ills, including the depression epidemic, high rates of stress, workplace dissatisfaction, and loneliness. The positive impacts of green choices on our lives go beyond these simple pleasures, to improving our long-term security and well-being. Lest you think it is just dreamy idealism to link eco-conscious living with personal and societal well-being, think about how good you feel when spending time outdoors or playing with a kitten. Many studies have noted the far-reaching positive aspects of making environmentally friendly choices.[184,185,186,187] And beyond personal gains and sending financial signals, your eco-friendly behaviors send stunningly effective social and political signals

Before we dive into the details of how to reduce our footprints, let's step back and ponder why 162 pounds of material are extracted from the Earth, every day, for every American.[188] Why are our lifestyles so resource-hungry that if everyone on the planet lived like the average American, we would need 5 Earths?[189] I think the answer lies in several aspects of modern culture: convenience and time saving, gratification, perceptions of security, and lack of knowledge. And underpinning it all, in my opinion, is our relationship with money and time. We perceive money as our primary source of security, and we consider ourselves as time-poor. So we use money to save time, even though earning that money uses up most of our time. Often the everyday decisions we make, like getting a take-away, saves us time, at the moment. But our spending choices are often a false economy. What I mean by that is that the time saved is usually outweighed by the total cost to our mental and physical health, our wallet, and our time. We have to work more to afford the perceived shortcut, and in doing so rob ourselves of a nurturing opportunity.

Now don't get me wrong. I would never argue that we shouldn't order take-away or eat out on occasion. Eating out can

---

[184] Hines, F. and K. Peattie 2006, "Critical review of data for environmental impacts of household activities: executive summary report", Cardiff, UK, BRASS Res. Cent.

[185] Tukker, A. 2006, "Environmental impacts of products: a detailed review of studies", J. Ind. Ecol. 10:159-82

[186] Spangenberg, J. and S. Lorek 2002, "Environmentally sustainable household consumption: from aggregate environmental pressures to priority fields of action", Ecol Econ. 43, 127-140.

[187] Peattie, K. 2010, "Green consumption: behavior and norms", Ann. Rev. Environ. Resour. 35: 195-228

[188] Schanel, H. et al 2016, Global Material Flows and Resource Productivity, Assessment Report for the UNEP International Resource Panel, ISBN: 978-92-807-3554-3

[189] Global Footprint Network 2016, https://www.footprintnetwork.org/ accessed July 15, 2019

be very joyous, and a take-away can be a huge relief. What's more, the ideas I present are not meant to be prescriptive: 'You must do this and not that.' Here, I mean only to offer thoughts and ideas about how to reduce our negative environmental impacts. Sorting out what you choose to do is obviously up to you. There are many paths. For instance, if you decide to eat fast food, perhaps you'll research which chains are the least destructive. A quick google search found a study that states that the very worst offenders in terms of environmental issues and workers rights were KFC, Little Caesars, Papa John's, Dominos, and Checkers, followed by Popeyes, Taco Bell, Wendy's, Sonic and Hardee's[190]. The best were In-N-Out, Chipotle, Starbucks, Panera Bread, Chick-Fil-A, Boston Market, Long John Silver's, Jason's Deli, Culver's, and Five Guys.[191] Food for thought.

To follow on from conclusions in the previous chapter that food and drink, transport, and the home account for 80% of natural resource depletion, I'll look at how one can reduce our own contributions to environmental damage from these three sectors. I'll also include a final section on plastic and summarize with a discussion of looking at these issues from a financial viewpoint. But as noted in the first paragraph of this chapter, the ideas presented below can be summed up a few simple rules of thumb: buy less, throw away less, and purchase wisely. I find it empowering to know that shifts in my consumption patterns significantly reduce my negative impacts, because these are things I can change. And of course, my choices also have ramifications up and down the political, financial, societal, and production chains.

## Improving the impact of the food we eat

In retrospect, it doesn't come as any surprise that of all our consumption categories, our food choices have the most significant negative impact on the planet. We all eat regularly, and

---

190 https://www.kcet.org/food/the-10-worst-fast-food-chains accessed January 28, 2019

191 https://www.kcet.org/food/the-10-best-fast-food-chains accessed January 28, 2019

food, unlike cars, houses, or clothes, is consumed daily. Furthermore, the higher up the food chain we go, the greater the environmental impact. To grow a crop of beans only requires one season, whereas to raise a cow requires feeding her over and over.

Similarly, the more special care a product needs, the more resources it will take - from greenhouses to storage to transport. So we already have a few rules of thumb to improve the environmental impact of our food: (a) reduce waste, (b) eat low down in the food chain, and (c) eat in-season, local, and organic foods. One rule to rule them all? Eat like a peasant. Maybe without the weevils.

## *Reduce Food Waste*

We throw away about 1/3 of the food we buy. Think of how much money we could each save if we didn't do this. Combined with what farmers destroy, driven in part by consumers' desire for perfect-looking food, about 1/2 of produced food is thrown away. That is an absurd waste. In terms of eco-impacts, it's disgraceful. There are many ways we can reduce food waste. Here are a few we can try:

- Menu plan
- Learn more about storing food (e.g., https://www.savethefood.com/food-storage)
- Learn about sell-by dates
- Learn about reviving wilted veg (e.g., pop wilted leaves in ice water for 10 minutes)
- Get creative with bits and pieces of food (e.g., https://www.lovefoodhatewaste.com)
- Buy wonky vegetables and other imperfect food items
- Prioritize meal preparation

This last one has been particularly poignant for me this year. Upon the realization that home food waste is such a huge contributor to all 8 of our essential natural resources, I've been trying hard not to waste food. So, I am endeavoring to see meal prep as the multi-layered social lever that it is. Meal prep impacts my budget, mealtime with the family, our health, and reduces my negative impact on freshwater supplies, biodiversity loss, wilderness loss, toxicant free environment, stable climate, and so forth. Granted, I'm not always successful, but I'm improving.

## *Reduce Meat and Dairy*

Since raising livestock is a significant cause of the depletion of 7 out of 8 of our natural resources, we must significantly change livestock production. As a species, we must minimize and alter livestock farming if we want to curtail biodiversity loss, damage to the oceans, deforestation, and soil losses. Everyone on the planet simply cannot eat as Americans do without invoking widespread environmental disasters with devastating consequences for humanity. The closer our food choices are to plants, the less negative environmental impact they have, for moving up the food chain requires more and more natural resources. So, for instance, it is less damaging to eat soybeans than it is to eat the chickens who are fed soybeans, over and over. Eating soy may sound dry and dull, but in fact, they are delicious if prepared simply. We learned to love them from the Japanese - blanched till warm and lightly salted - yum. My son, who spent his first three years in Japan and eschews all other green vegetables, will eat edamame like potato chips. They are great in packed lunches.

*Daily recommended amount of protein.* The first step we can all take to reduce our meat and dairy is to ensure we do not eat more than the daily recommended amount of protein. The USDA recommends that a 110-pound person consume 33 grams of protein a day, this is the amount of protein in a ¼ pound of ground beef. This daily protein recommendation is proportional to our weight, so for an average American at 185 pounds,[192] the recommended daily allowance is 65 grams of protein.[193] The most

---

192 https://www.cdc.gov/nchs/fastats/body-measurements.htm accessed August 26, 2019

193 *Dietary Reference Intakes for Energy, Carbohydrate, Fiber, Fat, Fatty Acids, Cholesterol, Protein, and Amino Acids* (2002/2005); and *Dietary Reference Intakes for Calcium and Vitamin D* (2011). www.nap.edu

recent estimate I could find about how many grams of protein the average adult American actually eats was from 2003-2004, which is 91 grams of protein a day.[194] So for health, and the planet, reducing our meat intake to recommended levels is an obvious first step.

*Vegetarian, vegan, and flexitarian options.* We can, of course, replace some of our meat dishes with vegetarian and vegan options. Plant-based diets free up even more land and are considered amongst the healthiest of diets resulting in lower risks of heart disease, type 2 diabetes, hypertension, certain types of cancer and obesity.[195] There are entire cuisines that are primarily vegetarian, and the variety and rich flavor in veggie/vegan dishes leave nothing wanting. Furthermore, meat substitutes have come a long way. I enjoy Morningstar's breakfast patties, Linda McCartney's mozzarella burgers, and Quorn chicken pieces. The latter of which makes a better fajita than chicken, perhaps because they absorb the marinade better. If you are opting for a simple kids' meal, meat-free chicken nuggets or fish sticks are far tastier than the over-processed meat versions, according to my young men.

There are many points along the animal restricted diet scale: veganism avoids all animal products, vegetarianism avoids meat, pescatarians avoid all meats except fish, and flexitarians eat meat and dairy occasionally. There are folks who eat vegan in January, Veganuary it's called, and folks who make a vegetarian meal from a meal kit once a week. Any reduction you make in your meat consumption is helpful - you don't have to give up meat all together. I consider myself a naughty vegetarian. While I have not eaten mammals for 32 years now, if someone cooks chicken or fish for me, I'll eat it. My first year as a naughty vegetarian I ate bacon because, well, it was bacon. Everyone has to choose their boundary. And if you're still struggling to make a meal without

[194] https://www.cdc.gov/nchs/fastats/body-measurements.htm accessed August 26, 2019

[195] Vesant, M., C. Winston and S. Levin, 2016, "*Position of the Academy of Nutrition and Dietetics: Vegetarian Diets*", Journal of the Academy of Nutrition and Dietetics 116, 1970.

meat, try a "Beyond Beef" burger. I had one recently and it was so like a real hamburger, I couldn't eat it. My meat-eating family tells me they are delicious.

When I set out to write this book, I had no idea I would reach the conclusion that reducing our meat intake is the single most effective thing we can do to protect our natural resources. It's not an easy sell. But it is an incontrovertible truth. If you eat meat, perhaps you could do so in light of it being a privilege, an actual treat rather than a run-of-the-mill kind of event. A meal to celebrate. Then if we are buying meat less often, we may be able to afford local organic meat rather than inexpensive factory-farmed meat as expanded on in the next sections.

## *Local, in Season, Whole Foods*

In addition to reducing our meat purchasing, we can also reduce our food's negative environmental impacts by eating local , in season, whole foods. I suspect the ecological benefits of local foods are obvious: less transport, less processing and packaging, and greater accountability. And of course, there are social benefits to buying local products like supporting small farms. To source local food, you can pay attention to food origin labels in the grocery store, attend farmers' markets, order a regular veg box from a local farmer, and - the pinnacle of local - grow your own. Local food generally tastes better because it can be harvested near to its optimal ripeness and isn't stored as long. We can also support restaurants that aim to follow these tenets.

A lot of local food will also be whole food - meaning a potato rather than frozen french fries - simply because not every community has food processing plants. Buying whole foods will also support our farmers, increasing their sales and profits if we buy directly from them. Of course, there are many health benefits to whole foods, and not just physical ones, but also mental health benefits, as seen in new links between our mental well-being and the health of gut flora.[196]

---

[196] Pennisi, E., 2019, "Evidence mounts that gut bacterian can influence mood, prevent depression", Science doi:10.1126/science.aaw9039

## *Organic Food*

Organic food production supports most of our 8 life-sustaining resources. In an organic garden, insects, plants, fungi, soil, and water are not inundated with various pesticides. Organic practices thus promote biodiversity and a toxicant free environment. For instance, the shocking decrease in insect numbers observed around the world in the past decades is likely, in large part, due to pesticide use.[197] Organic farming is literally grounded in supporting and protecting the soil resulting in dramatically healthier soil ecosystems. Plants grown in healthy soils are more resistant to crop losses from drought and floods, reducing water logging, irrigation, and pesticide. This helps prevent fresh and saltwater die offs and eutrophication. Organic farming even reduces climate change. Organically farmed soils store 28% more carbon than traditional industrial farming. If organic farming became widespread the soils would absorb an additional 11% of global carbon emissions every year for at least the next 20 years.[198] Finally, organic farms produce more crops per acre than industrial farms, over time, and therefore increase the area available for wilderness.[199] That's a pretty remarkable list of environmental benefits. There are also many health benefits to eating organic:

- Omega-3 fatty acids. Organic chicken has six times the healthy omega-3 fatty acid than a factory-farmed chicken. The majority of calories in factory-farmed chickens come from fat, not protein. Other organic meats, dairy, and eggs also have higher heart-healthy fat contents than non-organic equivalents.[200]

---

[197] Sánchez-Bayo, F. & K.A.G. Wyckhuys 2019 "Worldwide decline of the entomofauna: A review of its drivers", Biological Conservation 232, 8

[198] Soil Association 2009, "Soil carbon and organic farming: A review of the evidence of agriculture's potential to combat climate change"

[199] UN Human Rights Council 2017, *Report of the Special Rapporteur on the Right to Food*, https://documents-dds-ny.un.org/doc/UNDOC/GEN/G17/017/85/PDF/G1701785.pdf?OpenElement

[200] World Wildlife Fund 2017, *Appetite for Destruction*

- Anti-oxidants. Organic produce has small to moderate increases in certain types of flavonoids, which have antioxidant properties linked to reduced cancer and heart disease.[201]
- Toxic metal. Organic grains have lower cadmium levels when compared with conventionally grown ones.
- Pesticide residue. Organically grown produce has lower detectable levels of pesticides than conventional produce.
- Death. The UN estimates that 200,000 premature deaths are due to pesticides each year.
- Debilitation and disease. Long term exposure to pesticides is linked to cancer, Alzheimers and Parkinsons, hormone disruption, developmental disorders, sterility, higher rates of miscarriage and congenital disabilities, memory loss, loss of coordination, reduced sight and motor skills.[202]
- Bacteria. Organic meats have fewer occurrences of bacteria resistant to antibiotic treatment. The overall risk of bacterial contamination or food poisoning from organic and conventional foods are the same.[203]
- Taste. Organic and local veg taste better, as everyone who has enjoyed a sun-warmed tomato straight from the plant knows. Studies now confirm that fruit and veg which taste better have higher nutritional content.[204]

So, organic food is far better for us and the environment. What's not to like? The price, perhaps? Some organic foods are shockingly expensive, and undoubtedly, there are those of us who

---

[201] Mayo Clinic "Antioxidants: Why are they important", Accessed February 3, 2020 https://www.mayoclinic.org/healthy-lifestyle/nutrition-and-healthy-eating/multimedia/antioxidants/sls-20076428

[202] UN Human Rights Council 2017, *Report of the Special Rapporteur on the Right to Food,* A/HRC/34/48, Downloaded on October 10, 2018 from https://ap.ohchr.org/documents/dpage_e.aspx?m=101

[203] Mayo clinic article "Organic Foods: Are they safer? More nutritious?" Accessed August 27, 2019 https://www.mayoclinic.org/healthy-lifestyle/nutrition-and-healthy-eating/in-depth/organic-food/art-20043880?pg=2

[204]Breslin, P.A.S. 2013, "An Evolutionary Perspective on Food Review and Human Test, Cure Biol 6: 23 (9): R409-R48. Doi 10.1016/j.cub.2013.04.010

# *Figure 4.1 Improving the impacts of our eating habits*

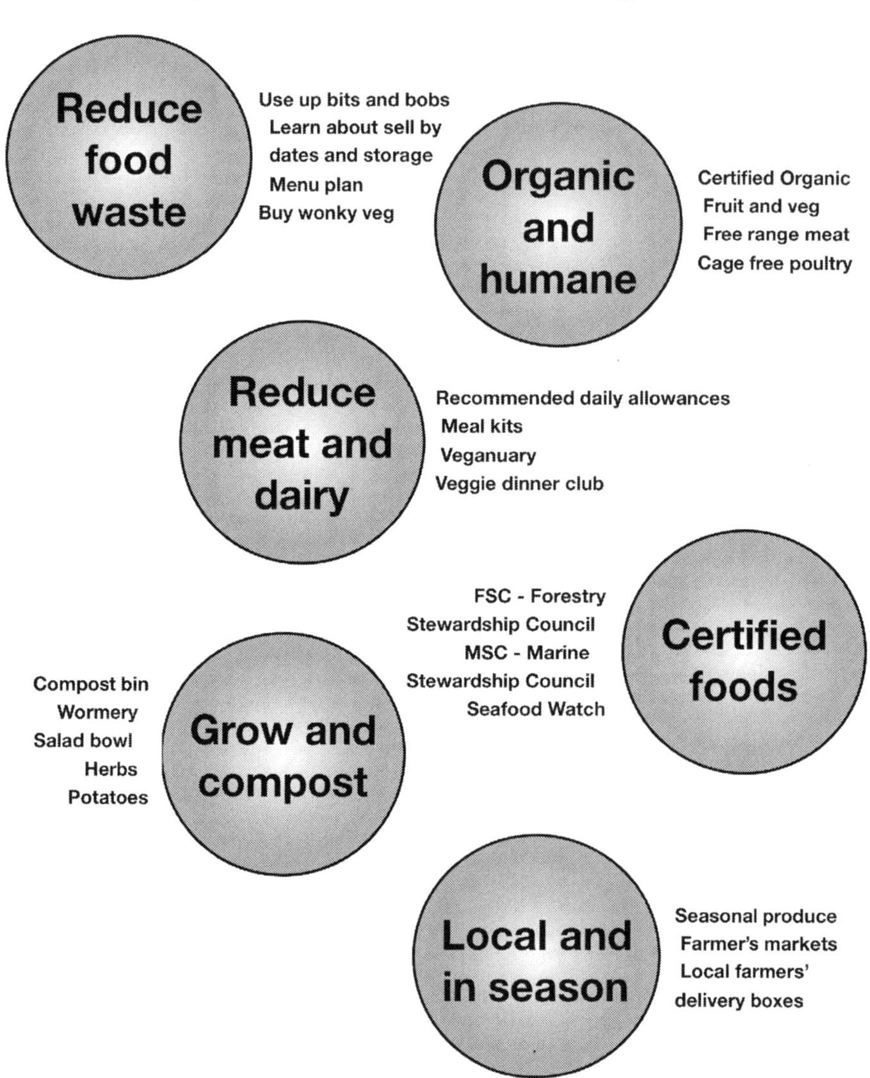


*Eat like a peasant, feel like a Queen*

simply can not afford to pay for organic products. But for those of us who can, or at least can do some of the time, buying organic goes a long way towards improving our environmental impacts. And let's remember the reason they cost so much. It takes human attention to grow organically, so again buying organic employs farmers. If we go further and buy local organic food, we are also helping to reduce wealth inequality and taking power from the multinational corporations. Food companies Nestle, Anheuser Busch, Pepsico, and Coca-cola rank 42nd, 69th, 86th, and 133rd in the listing of most powerful companies in 2019, according to Forbes Global ranking.[205]

## *"Certified" Foods*

How do we know if a food is actually organic? For a food to be labeled "Organic" or "100% Organic" in the U.S., they must have been *certified* as containing greater than 95% or 100% of organic ingredients, respectively. In this context, organic ingredients are those that comply with USDA's National Organic Program's certification process, including growth, handling, and production without pesticides or other synthetic chemicals, irradiation, or fertilizers made with synthetic ingredients, or lastly bioengineering. In addition, the and water health must be maintained.[206] It is, in fact, quite a rigorous process to achieve the right to label a product with the phrase "Certified Organic" or "Certified 100% Organic".

In addition to certified organic, there are a host of other ways food can be certified. Some of these can be controversial because there may still be negative environmental or social impacts in the production of the item. For my part, I am glad these controversies are brought to light and, also, that certification is carefully monitored. But I am happy to leave that monitoring to other people and support the certification process as much as I can when buying products. Here's a list of some of the certifications we can look for when buying stuff:

---

205 https://www.forbes.com/global2000/list/ Accessed August 27, 2019

206 https://www.ams.usda.gov/about-ams/programs-offices/national-organic-program

- FSC: Forestry Stewardship Council for paper products. Forest management and chain of custody.
- MSC: Marine Stewardship Council for fish. Sustainable fishing practices. There are also lists such as: https://www.thespruceeats.com/sustainable-seafood-choices-1665724 which examine overfishing and other issues and www.seafoodwatch.org.
- Certified Dolphin Safe: for tuna fish. Minimizes dolphins killed.
- Fair Trade. To protect workers who produce the product and often includes environmental considerations.
- "Certified organic" or "certified 100% organic".

## *Growing our Own*

Growing our own food is the penultimate in buying local products. And although I am a keen gardener, my veg patch is not so successful at feeding the family. However, it is a favorite foraging spot for the local birds, butterflies, moths, and other critters, and we enjoy the few products we do get. My marginally less paltry fruit trees and shrubs provide me with lots of fruit and also are enjoyed well into the autumn by the birds and bees. The one food group that I'm relatively successful with is herbs and salady things - mainly because these require the least attention. Mint is particularly easy to grow - though it can spread invasively, so perhaps put it in a pot and water when it looks sad. Another winner is salad leaves grown in a container. Lettuce germinates and grows quickly and is tasty when eaten fresh. I particularly like the cut-and-come-again varieties because I get extra harvests for the work of one planting.

## *Composting*

As a gardener, I treasure my compost pile because it helps me improve my soil, and I find the process of producing this garden gold fascinating. But composting also is a great thing to do for the environment. Rotting food at the dump releases a lot of methane gas, an estimated 3% of our greenhouse gases,[207]

---

[207] The Intergovernmental Panel on Climate Change 2014- The synthesis report of the 5 Assessment Report.

(IPCC 2014) whereas tossing food onto a compost pile doesn't - largely because there is more oxygen in contact with the decaying food. Furthermore, by having a compost pile we reduce transport costs and contributions to landfills, and we improve our local soil.

It's straightforward to have a compost pile. I have two piles. I fill up one of them with garden cuttings and any fruit or veg or eggs from the kitchen which haven't come in contact with any fats. Fats, like butter and oil, can attract rodents - so that goes in the garbage or if my town has it, the city compost. When one pile is 2 or 3 feet tall, I start on the next one. In a few months, I harvest the compost from the pile that has been fallow. Some people turn their compost piles, it speeds up decomposition. I don't. You can even skip the harvesting part and just pile up fruit and veg on a spot of soil or in a composting bin. I didn't empty my first plastic compost bin for eight years. When I did so, out of curiosity, I became a composting addict instantaneously because the humus was astoundingly rich and made my flowers grow like mad. And, no, compost piles don't smell, nor have I ever seen rodents in mine. If you are short of space, or don't have a garden, you could consider a wormery.

## Transportation: "Do the local-motion"

After food, transportation is the activity with the next greatest negative environmental impact. We can improve the impact of our own transportation as well as of the products we buy by concentrating on local activities and goods. Perhaps we could resurrect the 1960s hit song by Gerry Goffin and Carole King "Do the Loco-motion" as "Do the local-motion":

> *"Everybody's doing a brand-new dance, now*
> *Come on baby, do the local-motion*
> *I know you'll get to like it if you give a chance now*
> *Come on baby, do the local motion ….*
> *A little bit of rhythm and a lot of soul*
> *Come on, come on*
> *Do the local-motion with me."*

## *Walking*

When we live locally, it becomes easier to get to our destinations under our own power - walking or cycling. Much like with reducing our meat intake, any reduction in our driving is helpful. Walking and cycling have so many benefits beyond reducing air pollution, reducing the wear and tear on our car and the roads, and reducing greenhouse gas emissions. Until I researched this book, I considered walking the penultimate activity to 'save the world.' Now, I believe being conscientious about our food choices is our most impactful choice, but walking still holds a special place in my heart. Both activities are win/win/win habits - a win for you, for your neighborhood, and for larger society. Walking is good for your pocketbook and good for your physical and mental health while also addressing several environmental issues.

*Physical health benefits from walking.* You may have read that walking is about the best exercise there is. Our bodies were designed to walk a lot, and modern sedentary habits are counter to this. We get stiff and lethargic from sitting too much, and our muscles clench up and atrophy. Inactivity can lead to pain and more sitting around. I In my thirties, I suffered from such a bad back that I was bed-bound for months. I was diagnosed with a ruptured disc. I tried yoga, pilates, acupuncture, massage of various kinds, medicines, and chiropractic care, to name a few things. I was about to have surgery on my spine when I tried Dr. Sarno's advice and started walking.[208] Within two days, I was out of bed and walking around. But for several years, I couldn't walk far and was very limited in my activities. But then a three-month car-free life was forced on me after a move. Seriously annoyed, and anxious, I *had* to walk everywhere. We had two kids under the age of five at the time, so we had to get out of the house. I started slowly - just a few hundred yards at a time to the local park - and over the months, my back unwound, and now I can walk long distances confidently. Walking gave me my freedom and joy back. To those of us who can't physically walk, I'm sure I can't speak to your situation, but I hope you can access some of these benefits in alternative ways.

---

[208] Sarno, J.E. 1991, Healing Back Pain: The Mind-Body Connection, Warner Books

*Mental health benefits from walking.* There is nothing like a walk to clear your head. When we walk, we notice the weather and the seasons. We might even decide that a slight drizzle is fine walking weather or what began as a bitter cold walk ends as a bright, crisp invigorating winter adventure. Research has shown that walking alleviates our stress[209] and combats depression.[210] Walking also helps us solve problems by giving us space to daydream. The delightful book *The Organized Mind* talks about how we need to let our minds wander as it allows us to be creative and solve problems in ways that save us time in the end. I had a dramatic case of this when I was battling against a discrepancy in my master's research. I'd been working 60 plus hours a week for a couple of months, trying to sort it out, somewhat like smacking my head against a brick wall. I finally dreamt the answer. It felt like my brain was mildly disgusted with me for not seeing the solution and finally said "HERE, it's the Jacobian." Walking facilitates this daydreaming background processing, and had I partaken of it at that time, perhaps, I would have saved myself the stress, time, and sore head.

*The spiritual benefits of walking.* Many of the world's religions have walking traditions. You may know some: Buddhists have the ancient practice of walking meditation. Christians aim to walk with Christ and Muslims may go on pilgrimage by walking. But small religions have these traditions too: some native Americans have a spiritual practice of walking the four compass points, as in the Medicine Wheel, observing nature's signs and contemplating a complementary spiritual characteristic on each walk. Some indigenous tribes in Australia believe the world was created when creator-beings walked and sang and thus, one can navigate the land by following their songlines. Whatever you believe, walking can root us to the natural world and awaken our appreciation of the world around us.

*The societal benefits of walking.* When we walk in our neighborhoods, we build our community. We might wave at a

---

[209] https://www.ncbi.nlm.nih.gov/pubmed/10626033

[210] Roberston, R. et al 2012, "Walking for depression or depressive symptoms: A systematic review and meta analysis", *Mental Health and Physical Activity* 5, 1, 66-75

gardener, chat with a delivery person, or notice a blue jay's call. If we walk in our neighborhood regularly enough, we might make a new friend, connect with a lonely person, notice a change in wildlife, spot that someone's newspapers are piling up, or see a poster for an event we'd like to attend. You may learn how others are coping with an infestation on their tomato plants, or about a sale going on at the shoe store, or you may be able to ask your neighbor if you can borrow their lawn edger or snowblower. These may not be quantifiable achievements, but a strong community is important to everyone's welfare and is known to be very important for recovery following crises, as seen in the aftermath of Hurricane Katrina.[211]

*The knock-on environmental benefits of walking*. Of course, the most obvious eco-benefit to walking comes in reduced fossil fuel use, but regular walking also becomes part of one's entertainment and nurtures satisfaction. This reduces the likelihood that we'll go out and buy something else to entertain or satisfy ourselves. And because of the improvements in our physical and mental health brought about by walking, walking reduces the multifaceted costs of health care.

## *Living Locally*

Local living strengthens our local community by supporting local businesses, developing social networks, and enhancing local knowledge and local solutions to problems. All of the embodied energy in producing cars and trucks, buses and trains, airplanes, roads, and services are reduced when we reduce the miles of transportation needed to support our lives. You may think that because the streets and your car already exist, you might as well use them. But cars and roads will be worn out more quickly the more we use them, and our continued reliance on them makes it harder for large scale change to occur. It's interesting to think about living locally in terms of the different aspects of our lives: work, school, clubs, friendships, food, utilities, family, and worship are just a few. The simple act of chatting with a local can expand our social bubble, exchange ideas and strengthen our community.

[211] Chamlee-Wright, E., 2010, "The cultural and political economy of recovery: Social learning in a post-disaster environment", Routledge

I find it very straightforward and satisfying to live locally in my day-to-day life. Whenever possible, I choose services to which I can walk. I try to make trips part of the day's activities - perhaps I'll cycle to a friend's and count that as my exercise. However, I struggle with long-distance travel to visit family. Recently, my sister came to England and stayed with me for five weeks. It was fabulous and sated our sister-time-need for a while. So perhaps longer, less frequent visits are part of the answer to my long-distance visits. I used to travel a great deal for work. At one point, I decided I wouldn't fly anymore to attend meetings. That hurt my career, my ego, and my fun quota! I'm not sure what is right regarding work travel, but I reckon we should all be very choosy about travel and support those who limit their travel.

### *Making the most of trips*

This one is pretty obvious, isn't it? We can combine errands, so we take fewer trips to different parts of town. If you tend to travel for holidays, perhaps take a longer one away from home this year and have a local holiday next year. We can also combine our trips with other people - see if your new gardening friend fancies sharing a trip to the plant nursery or if your neighbor would like to share rides to the grocery store. You can always start slowly and see how it works, such as commuting together once a week.

## Home energy, buildings and appliances

This is the last of the three most significant environmental impact consumption categories. A small number of activities make up the vast majority of the impacts of this group. In particular, heating, construction and maintenance, and appliances dominate this group's eco-effects.[212]

At 43% of home energy usage, heating our houses is the biggest home energy category. Water heating accounts for an additional 19% and air conditioning 8%, making these three

[212] Tukker, A. et al 2006, Environmental Impact of Products (EIPRO) , European Commission Joint Research Centre EUR 22284 EN.

categories together more than 70% of home energy usage.[213] Therefore, insulating our homes, putting up curtains or multiple glazed windows, moderating the temperature on the thermostat, and closing off rooms we are not using are all very effective at reducing overall household energy use. When installing a new heating/cooling system, it is worth considering geothermal heat pumps or solar water heating, which tend to have higher installation costs but save money within some 5-10 years following installation. There are also some tax credits and rebates available in many places for installing renewable energy sources.[214]

We can also learn to cope with lower temperatures in our homes and offices during the winter, saving energy and money, as well as having health benefits. Living in a cooler house means we burn more calories to stay warm; and we have to get up and be active every hour or two to warm ourselves up. Low room temperatures can even reduce inflammation.[215] I wear two layers and sport a dandy wooly cap much of the winter, which is no hardship and sure to amuse the teenagers.

As for reducing our hot water usage, we can do many things. It has been shown time and again that washing clothes at 30°C gets them just as clean as washing at 60° or higher. We can limit our shower time - for each shower or by not showering daily, which is so much better for our skin. And as for washing dishes, it is very effective to fill a bowl with hot sudsy water and wash in batches, only turning on the tap to rinse a bunch at a time. As someone who is always conscious of water usage, this practice actually relaxes me because then I am not rushing through the washing up to reduce my water usage.

The construction and maintenance of our homes contribute to our homes' environmental impact. In addition to energy, the use of resources to build our homes and to fit it with appliances,

---

213 US Energy Information Administration, https://www.eia.gov/todayinenergy accessed August 29, 2019
http://needtoknow.nas.edu/energy/energy-efficiency/heating-cooling/

214 State: https://www.energy.gov/savings/search Federal: https://www.energystar.gov/about/federal_tax_credits

215 Klein, S.2015, "6 surprising health benefits of cold weather", The Huffington Post, https://www.huffpost.com/entry/health-benefits-cold-weather_n_2528779 accessed August 30, 2019

lighting, and plumbing all have ecological consequences. As I know very little about these aspects, I gleaned the suggestions in Figure 4.2 below from the website of Carnevale Eustis Architects.[216]

| Figure 4.2 Sustainable building features | | |
|---|---|---|
| Site | Construction | Building Interior |
| • Retain and reuse existing buildings<br>• Locate new buildings to minimize the impact on site<br>• Protect native plants<br>• Rainwater cisterns for toilets and irrigation<br>• Dark Sky compliant exterior lighting | • Geothermal HVAC<br>• "Cool" metal roofs<br>• Roof overhangs for shading<br>• Solar panels<br>• Insulation<br>• Thick walls to maximize insulation<br>• Formaldehyde-free building sheathing<br>• Low E insulated glass<br>• Skylights / daylighting | • Compact fluorescent light bulbs<br>• Occupancy sensor light switches<br>• Renewable flooring materials<br>• Low flow plumbing fixtures<br>• "Energy Star" appliances<br>• Low/no VOC paints |

In addition to building considerations, there are two aspects of owning and running appliances in our homes that we can consider: energy usage and resources needed to build and dispose of / recycle a product. Taken all together, this is called the embodied impact and can be estimated with a so called lifecycle analysis. It is easy to find estimates of the first aspect of the embodied impact: energy usage. For an average American home, lighting uses 7.2% of the home electricity budget, fridge/freezers 6.3%, washer, dryers, and dishwashers 5%, TVs 4.2%, cooking

216 https://www.cearchitects.com/about-carnevale-eustis-architects.php

*Reducing appliance impacts*

Purchasing alternatives
- Borrow
- Rent
- Repair
- Do without

Purchasing considerations
- Energy efficient products
- High quality appliances
- Repairable units
- Multipurpose tools
- Recyclability

appliances 2.7%, computers 1.6%, and 20.8% in a miscellaneous category.[217] We can save electricity and money, by purchasing energy-efficient products and by using them less. Appliances with the *Energy Star* certification saved US families and businesses 30 billion dollars, and 400 kilowatt hours of electricity in 2016.[218]

It is more challenging to rank appliances and other products in terms of their production and disposal costs. One product may use few resources but concentrate a toxic chemical, such as in many batteries, whereas another product may be wholly organic but require acres of land to produce. When we do buy a product, it can be useful to consider the following questions: How useful is it? Can it be used for lots of jobs or just one? Is it repairable if it breaks down? How long will it last? Can it be recycled when it is no longer useful?

There is a more radical option than buying green products. That is not buying the product at all. You can consider borrowing from a neighbor, renting an appliance or tool, or buying second hand. In some instances, you may find you don't need specific products. In the three places we lived in England, we didn't have a microwave, a clothes dryer, or a dishwasher. Doing without these appliances was never an issue - in fact, it was less to clean,

[217] National Academy of Sciences, Engineering and Medicine, What you need to know about Energy: Energy Efficiency website accessed February 25, 2019 http://needtoknow.nas.edu/energy/energy-efficiency/heating-cooling/

[218] https://www.energystar.gov/about accessed February 27, 2019

maintain, and have repaired. Less clutter. The clothes dryer is probably the most effective appliance to do without, for it uses a considerable amount of energy, and using it drastically reduces the lifetime of your clothes. By not buying appliances, and not running them, we can reduce the depletion of our 8 natural resources.

## Plastic

While plastic usage is not generally one of the categories which features in studies of consumption impacts, its ubiquity in the modern world poses some severe health and environmental problems. I have therefore included this special section focusing on plastic and summarised it in *Figure 4.3 Plastic*. Where should we start? Plastic is everywhere in modern life. It is so useful and has immediate environmental and economic benefits by making objects less expensive to move around and in preserving food.

However, plastic's production consumes 8% of the global oil supply.[219] Plastic has been found in even the most remote ecosystems, where it damages wildlife. Ninety percent of us have leached plastic chemicals in our bloodstream.[220] We do not know plastic's long-term effects on the environment or ourselves. We don't even know about plastic's durability as it was only invented in the 1950s. Estimates for how long it takes for a plastic bottle to degrade range from 500 to 1000 years. Even when plastic degrades, we don't know if it will return to its original parts or just crumble into smaller pieces of plastic. That's worrying because small plastic particles can cross cell walls and have been shown to interfere with hormone levels affecting reproduction, liver and kidney function, and neurological processes.[221] Taken together with its ubiquity and its durability, that's downright chilling.

---

[219] UNEP 2014, Valuing Plastics: The Business Case for Measuring, Managing and Disclosing Plastic Use in the Consumer Goods Industry.

[220] WebMD Accessed June 4, 2020, "The facts about Bisphenol A", https://www.webmd.com/children/bpa#1

[221] Rochman, C et al 2013, "Ingested plastic transfers hazardous chemicals to fish and induces hepatic stress", Nature Scientific Reports 3, Article number: 3263

We produce 311 million tonnes of plastic a year. And because it doesn't degrade until centuries have passed, it is piling up. And not just in landfills. Thirty-five percent of plastic packaging, which represents ¼ of all plastic production, becomes litter. Only 5% of plastic packaging is recycled, in part because of the many kinds of plastic and plastic additives. The fact that only a small amount of plastics are recovered means that we throw away 80-120 billion US dollars in plastic packaging every year. When we add to this the cost of cleaning it up, plastic litter costs about 150 billion US dollars a year.[222] That's about half of what the UN estimates it would take to end world hunger.[223]

There is so much plastic litter in the ocean, that there are islands of plastic in the Pacific the size of Texas. If trends continue, we expect there to be more plastic by weight than fish in the oceans by 2050.[224] There are an estimated 14,000 pieces of plastic litter in every square kilometer of the ocean, meaning there are 50 times more pieces of plastic in the seas than there are stars in our galaxy.

Macroplastic, stuff we see, is ingested by and entangles sea life. Sea mammals, reptiles, birds, and fish become entangled in fishing nets with one study showing well over 50% of humpback whales show scars from entanglement with fishlines. Many of us will have seen the photos of whale stomachs, choked with 1000 pounds of plastic, and albatrosses, whose bodies have decayed to expose softball-size clumps of plastic in their stomachs. The physical blockages caused by plastic are sometimes lethal, while lesser damage may weaken an animal, so it succumbs to other threats. If plastic is ingested, chemical damage to cells of the kidney, liver, brain, and placenta can occur.

We do not know the human health implications of so much plastic. But we do know macro plastic, stuff we see as litter, acts as a breeding place for vector-borne diseases such as the Zika

---

[222] Ellen MacArthur Foundation and McKinsey & Company, The New Plastics Economy — Rethinking the future of plastics

[223] FAO,IFAD and WFP. 2015. Achieving Zero Hunger: the critical role of investments in social protection and agriculture, ROME, FAO

[224] Ellen MacArthur Foundation and McKinsey & Company, The New Plastics Economy — Rethinking the future of plastics

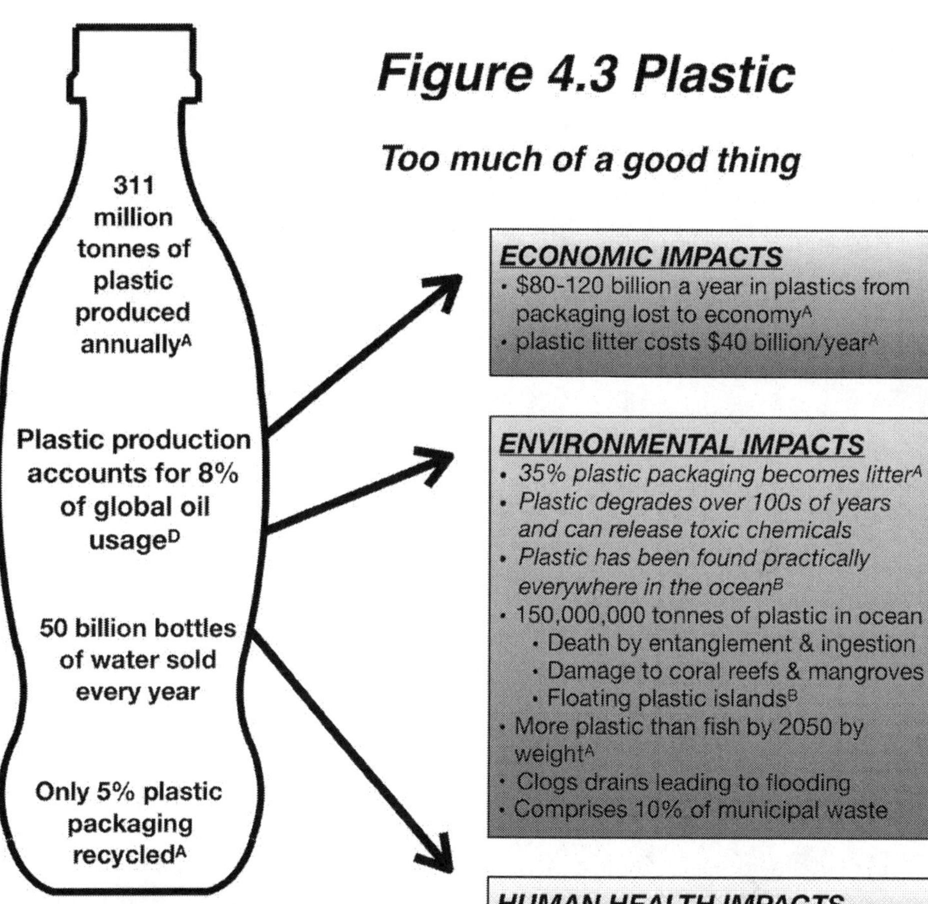


**Figure 4.3 Plastic**

***Too much of a good thing***

***HUMAN HEALTH IMPACTS***

- *Vector for diseases and bacteria*
- *Potential neurological damage from plastics in food*[B]
- *BPA, which leaks from drink bottles into water, results in cancer, liver, kidney, & reproductive damage in animals.*[B] *More than 90% of us have BPA in blood*[C]
- *Nanoplastics (tiny plastic bits) can cross human cell walls and effect immune system, fibrosis, gut ephithelium, inflammation and cell damage*[B]

WHAT WE CAN DO

- Refuse plastic bottles & straws
- Reduce plastic bag / packaging
- Use bar soap rather than liquid
- Learn more & talk about it
- Manage our waste
- Opt for natural fibres
- Support plastic taxes or bans

*A. Ellen MacArthur Foundation and McKinsey & Company, The New Plastics Economy — Rethinking the future of plastics B. UNEP (2016). Marine plastic debris and microplastics – Global lessons and research to inspire action and guide policy change. C. WebMD Accessed June 4, 2020, "The facts about Bisphenol A", https://www.webmd.com/children/bpa#1 D. UNEP (2014) Valuing Plastics: The Business Case for Measuring, Managing and Disclosing Plastic Use in the Consumer Goods Industry.*

virus. Micro-plastic, less than 1 millimeter across (0.04 inches), transport bacterial infections and has been found in human brains and placentas impacting on the immune system and leading to fibrosis, gut problems, inflammation, and cell damage.Smaller yet is nano plastic, which is less than 0.001 millimeters (0.00004 inches) across. Nano plastic can leak from packaging into food and drinks and once in our bodies is known to cross cell walls and cause neurological and other organ damage. Ninety percent of us have the plastic additive BPA in our bloodstream, which is known to result in liver, kidney, and reproductive damage in lab animals.[225], [226]

How do we go about reducing our plastic usage? Number one has to be avoiding using single use plastics like plastic drink bottles, grocery bags and over packaged food. We can use bar soap, tinfoil, and reusable food storage containers. We can frequent shops and restaurants which have similar aims to reduce plastic usage. We can bring our own mug to the coffee shop. With 50 billion plastic bottles of water alone sold every year, reducing plastic drinking bottles would be a good start and show the industry we are serious.

## Simple and effective win / win / win habits

This chapter includes many suggestions for reducing our negative environmental impacts. In the box "Simple and effective win / win / win habits", on the opposite page, I list habits that are simple, ecologically responsible, and yield a multitude of other benefits. These kinds of changes to our habits scale-up across social sizes, from the individual to the community, right up to national and global impacts. Our eco-choices also send economic and political signals, as well as improving our physical or mental health. Because this set of actions has positive impacts on social-commercial-personal issues, as well as individual-community-

---

225 UNEP 2015, Biodegradable Plastics and Marine Litter. Misconceptions, concerns and impacts on marine environments. United Nations Environment Programme, Nairobi

226 WebMD, Accessed June 4, 2020, "The facts about Bisphenol A", https://www.webmd.com/children/bpa#1

## Simple and effective win/win/win habits

For you, nature, community, justice, peace and the future

***Walk places:*** frequent a local shop or park on foot
***Reduce meat consumption:*** eat more chocolate
***Eat local, whole, organic foods:*** join a veg box scheme
***Reduce food waste:*** menu plan
***Reduce plastic usage:*** stop using plastic drink bottles
***Reduce garbage production:*** buy less
***A regular vegan night:*** sign up for a weekly meal kit
***Live locally:*** talk to your neighbor
***Reduce energy usage:*** line dry your clothes
***Reduce carbon footprint:*** get a green energy provider
***Reduce paid work:*** have time to budget, cook, repair
***Smell the roses:*** sniff
***Finances:*** ethical banking and investments

## Positive outcomes of win/win/win habits

Decreased natural resource use
Increased physical and mental health
Improved wealth diversification
More equal wealth distribution
Greater community resilience
Improved intergenerational justice
Political & monetary signals
Influence social norms
Develop eco-habits
Become an effective eco-conscious consumer

global impacts, I call them win / win / win habits. In other words, these are behaviors which will make us happier and healthier, protect our natural resources, and strengthen our communities, all whilst sending out those political, monetary, and social signals. That's a powerful punch for one straightforward switch.

If you do some of these already, fantastic. Try another? If you don't yet, maybe you will try one of these lifestyle choices. And when we do, let's celebrate that. Maybe you'll work to reduce your food waste. If so, well done. You may start taking a daily walk. That's huge! Who knows the implications of that walk. Perhaps you'll talk about local veg box schemes to a friend and influence them, or maybe you or your friend will come back and change something else a year from now. Maybe you'll make a new friend on your walk. But even if you simply stop contributing to the millions of plastic drinks bottles which are thrown away every day, this is a life-affirming step - which is also good for your pocketbook, your health, and your community. I find that as I adopt more of these habits, I feel more comfortable with my lifestyle, more peaceful, healthier, and happier. I think it is because then I know that I am doing my bit, I'm being responsible about my impact on the wilderness and social networks. I find being eco-active has a similar invigorating and healthy feel to improving my physical fitness.

## What influences our choices?

Even when we know something is good for us, let alone good for nature, it can be challenging to stick to a plan. So what might make us stick to ethical consumption? In a comprehensive review, researcher Peattie[227] looked at many past research studies and found there were 13 commonly studied influences on green consumer choices. The results would be surprising to many people who consider themselves quite eco-conscious and suggests more humility may be helpful when said people discuss consumption patterns.

---

[227] Peattie, K. 2010, "Green consumption: Behavior and norms", Annu Rev. Environ. Resour. 35: 195-228, 10.1146/annurev-environ-032609-094328

First of all, green consumption tends to be quite hit and miss with most people engaging in a little bit of it, but not in every aspect of their life. And secondly, many of the influences which are often focused on by environmental advocates have limited impact and sometimes even negative ones. For instance, things like environmental knowledge, economic considerations, demographics, values, and community structure (eg, rural versus urban) are not that influential when it comes to making green choices. A stark example is that environmental knowledge, rather than being the golden ticket to ensuring eco-activity, can lead to confusion and abandonment of eco-efforts by an individual. I probably run that risk in this book, which is why I've included the win-win-win options and the rules of thumb, like the cheeky 'Eat like a peasant' suggestion.

What does make a big difference in consumption choices are more subtle aspects of identity and community. These important influences include an individual's sense of self and their community. This is an important reason why adopting one eco-conscious habit can have profound effects on yourself and your neighbors. The following most strongly influence the adoption of eco-friendly practices:

- *Perceived responsibility and effectiveness.* A perception of shared responsibility for environmental problems and the belief that one's behavior has an impact.
- *Identity.* Consumers who self-identify as environmentally aware.
- *Lifestyle and habits.* The power of habit is such that day-to-day behaviors become locked in rather than considered in light of values, identity, environmental knowledge, etc. The time, energy, and financial barriers to adopting new habits are therefore critical.
- *Social norms and processes.* We tend to adopt 'normal' behavior rather than alternative behavior. We do what people in our home, neighborhood, church, workplace, country, and so forth are doing.[228]

---

[228] Peattie, K. 2010, "Green consumption: Behavior and norms", Annu Rev. Environ. Resour. 35: 195-228, 10.1146/annurev-environ-032609-094328

These findings and logic both suggest that the first step to engaging in eco-conscious behaviors is a belief that we have a responsibility to other living beings - be those human or otherwise. Once we acknowledge that we have an obligation to others, and we understand the impacts of our lifestyles, eco-conscious behaviors may then be viewed as a moral obligation. But it is also crucial that we feel that changing our practices will be effective. I hope that this book has ignited or strengthened your conviction that our consumption patterns are effective and critical levers for positive environmental impacts.

The next eco-behavior influencer identified by Peattie was seeing oneself as eco-conscious. I think most of us do act to reduce our negative environmental impacts, to one extent or another. However, the most usual societal perception seems to link being green to being liberal and even on occasion to being feminine.[229] Being eco-conscious is not owned by the left. No one likes to see pointless waste, and we all hate to see animals suffering. Anyone may identify as eco-conscious. Male. Female. Left. Right. Green or purple. As I argued in the forward to this book, many of the great conservationists have been, and continue to be, republicans. It would be fantastic if, through the loving work of protecting the environment, we could heal some of the left-right wounds. Acknowledging a desire to preserve the wilderness and prevent the suffering of financially needy people may be the most important step in your eco-conscious path this year. No matter what your political stance, I encourage you to embrace the eco-rebel within.

If we identify as an eco-conscious, then eco-habits are no longer a burden but instead blossom into an opportunity to do good work. When we switch from viewing something as a negative which we must undertake, 'I must go running' to a positive 'I get to go running,' our whole experience of the activity changes. I feel this more about running as my body ages, and I'm grateful for the days I can go running. Ha! Wisdom in creakiness.

---

[229] Hunt, E. 2020 "The eco-gender gap: Why is saving the planet seen as women's work?", https://www.theguardian.com/environment/2020/feb/06/eco-gender-gap-why-saving-planet-seen-womens-work, accessed February 6, 2020

When I see running as a choice, I can celebrate that it makes me feel good, helping my body and decluttering my mind. There are many parallels between this running example and eco-conscious choices. You may find, as I do, that clawing back consumption reduces the feelings of bloatedness, unease, and guilt over how much stuff is consumed. Just as we find with exercise, if we have a habit, we are more likely to engage in the activity. The more we do something, the more likely we are to do it in the future.

Social norms are also important factors in whether or not we engage in eco-conscious patterns. This is part of the power of being green: making eco-choices influences those around us. Our droplet of impact ripples outward. By reducing how much we buy, we are pushing back against materialism. We know this is a good thing to do, of course, but it is difficult to enact sometimes. Many of us believe that it is financially responsible to choose which product to buy based primarily on the cost in dollars. But when we do this, we ignore other moral considerations. For me, it is helpful to remember a single rule, like 'buy the cheapest product', is problematic. A non-green product may cost less for me, in terms of money, but it is likely to cost far more for society in terms of environmental damage. Of course, oftentimes, the green choice is to buy nothing, and that does save money.

In my opinion, eco-conscious choices are a profound societal obligation. Rather than following the 'business as usual' practice of using natural resources to save our time and money, we need to turn it around and use our time and money to save natural resources. When I had a paid job and was time-poor, we used our money to buy eco-friendly products as much as possible. Now that I'm at home writing, I use some of my time to fix things, grow food and medicines, and search for new solutions to family needs. These are two different eco-living options spanning time rich / cash poor to time-poor / cash-rich. Some folks, however, are both cash and time poor. I would suggest that these folks are far less of an environmental burden on the planet than the more financially wealthy. The less affluent simply can't buy as much stuff and they will presumably be far more resourceful in terms of fixing things or borrowing an uncommonly used tool. The less wealthy have sustainability practices hardwired into their economics. If you are not both cash and time-poor then, in my opinion, you are beholden to other beings to be careful of how you consume.

And while on the topic of finances, we could prioritize our sustainability efforts on those activities for which we spend the most money. It is probably a good rule of thumb that the relative amount of expenditure in our budgets is a proxy for which expense has the most significant environmental impact, be it positive or negative. For my family, our mortgage is 28% of post-tax income, food is 18%, and utilities are 16%. The remaining 38% is made up of miscellaneous things like running the car, repairing the house, visiting family, and shoveling cash at teenagers.

Perhaps, the most eco-effective thing I could do would be to look at our mortgage. Is it with an ethical bank? The reason it is so vital that we use ethical financial institutes is, of course, because banks support much of development. So if you feel strongly about any moral issue, you may wish to know your bank, pension, or investment portfolio's track record for that issue. For instance, I don't want my bank to support eco-destructive practices like deforestation or poor labor practices. A quick check of our mortgage[230] shows my bank is in the lowest category for these ethics. Yuck.

There's an informative article here[231] about banks in the US that have been certified by an independent board as adhering to social and environmental practices. These certifications, including B Corp Businesses and The Global Alliance for Banking on Values, are the fair trade of the banking world. It seems to me that the responsible eco-warrior would invest a couple of days to sort out 28% of their monetary influence in the world. For once done, having an ethical mortgage will have a long-lasting effect on their right to be smug. I'm missing a trick here. But seriously, I am reminded that I'd like to look at remortgaging. A few days of researching and paperwork, will turn 28% of our family's financial influence to good, for years to come. Now that's a good return.

---

230 https://thegoodshoppingguide.com/ethical-mortgages accessed August 12, 2019

231 https://www.nerdwallet.com/blog/banking/socially-responsible-banks/#list accessed August 12, 2019

# 5 THE DEEP CONNECTIONS BETWEEN SOCIAL AND ENVIRONMENTAL ISSUES

## The societal obligation to protect natural resources

Environmental degradation has grave social ramifications. The world's poor rely more directly on the land because natural resources often underpin their livelihood, food sources, and health care. Ecosystem services are estimated to account for 75% of the GDP for the poor in Indonesia, 47% for India's poor, and 89% for Brazil's. Furthermore, those with less money are far more vulnerable to natural disasters, crop failures, and floods, for they have less financial capital to prepare, respond, and adapt to crises. Between 2008 and 2012, 97% of global mortality from natural disasters occurred in low and lower-middle-income countries. The poor also tend to benefit the least from natural resource extraction, for they own less of the land.[232] Therefore, preserving natural resources is not just about other species, ourselves, or our children's futures. It is also about social justice today. It is about respecting the needs of less wealthy people - allowing them to live healthy and prosperous lives.

In the other direction, poverty can exacerbate environmental destruction. The lack of access to infrastructure, education, and money can make it impossible to participate in

[232]United Nations Development Programme and Unite Nations Environment Programme 2015, "Mainstreaming Environment and Climate for Poverty Reduction and Sustainable Development", available online at www.unpei.org

eco-conscious practices. Without access to water or energy sources, knowledge about best practice or mitigation strategies, the poor can and do turn to natural resources as a direct income source, potentially exacerbating environmental degradation, which leads to more poverty and back around again. Indeed the circular links between the environment and poverty are so strong that 193 nations have adopted the United Nations' (UN) document *The Future We Want*. This report states that the ***only viable path to sustainable development integrates economic, social and environmental dimensions.***[233] The UN General Assembly adopted an integrated approach in 2015, articulated in the 17 Sustainable Development Goals. This approach acknowledges the interdependency of eradicating hunger and poverty, fostering peace and justice, and protecting ecosystems.[234] To paraphrase the World Wildlife Fund we can not lift people out of poverty if we don't protect the environment, and we can't protect the environment without alleviating the impacts of poverty.[235]

I have heard it argued that we should be concentrating on helping people rather than the environment. And while I disagree, because I think all beings have a right to a chance at life and a touch of the divine in them, I can respect the humans-first point of view. However, pollution, loss of forests and coral reefs, and dried up rivers already severely degrade the quality of life of many of the world's less cash-rich. If we want humanity to survive and thrive, in the coming decades and centuries, we need to protect our natural resources. With a business-as-usual future, environmental problems will only get more drastic and more frequent as demonstrated by increasing numbers of droughts, and floods, and more intense hurricanes and fires in recent years.

---

***233*** United Nations General Assembly 2012, "The Future We Want", https://sustainabledevelopment.un.org/futurewewant.html

234 Mainstreaming Environment and Climate for Poverty Reduction and Sustainable Development: The Interactive Handbook to Strengthen Planning and Budgeting Processes, Published November 2017 accessed online at www.unpei.org/about-the-interactive-handbook March 8, 2019.

235 World Wildlife Fund accessed March 8, 2019. https://www.wwf.org.uk/what-we-do/projects/fighting-poverty-and-making-development-sustainable

Presumably, we can all agree enhanced hardship for the sake of unnecessary consumption is not just. And even in the immediate interest of those who are financially well off, eco-conscious choices can help to solve a myriad of modern-day social ills. In the following, I argue that by challenging some of our socially accepted conventions, we can go a long way toward solving both environmental and social issues.

## Social conventions which contribute to greater resource use

I've been concerned about the impact of modern life on nature all my life. Our impact on the natural world is never far from my mind. It creeps in at every decision and permeates my conversations. I am often thinking of the whys, the hows, and the whats of nature conservation from which peanut butter to buy to what job to pursue. Of particular interest to me has always been the question of why we consume so much. It is remarkable to me that from a broad array of viewpoints, covering various issues, conversations converge on the idea that a common set of social conventions underpin our ever increasing consumption.The following seem to underlie increasing consumption trends: I. Rising material expectations, II. Increasing levels of perceived independence, and III. A blinkered focus on paid work. What do I mean by these, and why do I think they are pivotal in our efforts to protect our natural resources? I'm glad you asked.

### *Rising Material Expectations*

I reckon it is self-evident that the more we expect to own, the more we're likely to buy. We hope to live longer, to be better off, and to be able to buy and do more than previous generations. Most of us have more clothes than we need. Nearly all of us in the US and Britain over the age of 15 have a cell phone. Many of us have individual computers and/or tablets. We have an astonishing array of tools and appliances. And most of us live in our own homes, rented, mortgaged, or owned, apart from the extended family. Previous generations didn't expect to possess nearly as much as we do. These are the classic signs of what we think of as economic well-being, i.e., economic growth. However, these growing expectations come hand-in-hand with higher material demands.

Hopefully, Chapter 2 convinced you that we can not continue using up natural resources at the current rate, let alone continue to grow our material consumption. The UN estimates that global material extraction has tripled between 1970 and 2010 to a staggering 22 billion tonnes of primary materials dug out of the earth every year. Over this time, the global population has only doubled, meaning per capita extraction has increased by 50%. North Americans have the highest per capita extraction at 25 tonnes a year. That's 55,000 pounds per person per year, over 150 pounds a day. The average African's material extraction rate is less than one eighth of that.[236]

As we've seen in Chapter 2, the result of this extraction is a dramatic depletion in our natural capital. If consumption continues at current rates, we will have severe shortages of fresh air, fresh water, biodiversity, and soil. Environmental depletion leads to famines, droughts, pollution, ecosystem collapses, and likely resource wars. What's more, population and per capita material use are both on increasing trajectories. I would never argue that we abandon the strive for a healthier and happier life. Still, we do need to challenge our perception that health and well-being are reliant on more and more stuff. The UN also argues that we need to decouple economic growth from material extraction.[237] We can contribute to this decoupling by valuing and prioritizing non-monetary wealth. We can value and prioritize the wealth that is good health, opportunities, strong communities, natural resources, meaningful work, skills, and knowledge. Arguably, these are far more important to security than money as anyone who has ever lost their health knows very well. I don't like to state 'musts' and 'shoulds', but if we want social or intergenerational justice and healthy places to live, we must consume fewer

[236]United Nations Environment Programme, 2016. Global Material Flows and Resource Productivity. An Assessment Study of the UNEP International Resource Panel. Paris.

[237] UNEP (2016) Global Material Flows and Resource Productivity as above

material goods. Reducing consumption, in turn, relies on adjusting our material expectations.

## *Greater Perceived Independence and Tribalism*

The second social trend which contributes to increased consumption is our growing perception of autonomy. The ongoing growth of the economy means many of us can afford our own stuff. Therefore we don't knock on the neighbor's door to ask to borrow their hedge trimmer, instead we buy our own. Many of us have our own sets of carpentry tools, screens to watch, cars to drive, and so forth. We drive into town rather than beg a cup of sugar off the neighbor. And as our neighbors do the same, the idea of asking someone to lend a hand becomes alien to us. We feel we would be bothering them. We start to feel self-reliant. And this the perception of increasing self-reliance leads to more resource use: I need my own table saw, my own car, my own computer, my own house. This trend unwittingly leads to greater social isolation.

Alongside our growing perceived independence, we are all moving more frequently, making families more geographically dispersed and disrupting long-term friendships and acquaintances. Social networks are moving away from neighbors and family to interest-oriented groups -- be these hobby, work-related, or spiritual groups. We are becoming more tribal. Research shows that we tend to only socialize with like-minded people, we are less likely to interact with neighbors, and we join fewer organizations and clubs than several decades ago.[238] In the US, at least, we trust one another less and trust the government far less than in previous decades.[239] This lack of trust is hamstringing our ability to fix problems, perhaps most notably at the national level.

News media, politics, and even family gatherings are fraught with left/right tensions. We don't trust what the other side says. Some folk don't trust religious leaders, some don't trust scientists, some don't trust environmentalists. There are undoubtedly examples of dishonest democrats, republicans,

---

[238] Putnam, R. 2000, Bowling Alone, Simon and Schuster, New York

[239] Helliwell, J. et al 2017 "The World Happiness Report 2017"

pastors, activists, and scientists, but the vast majority of them mean well. If we can't listen gracefully and respectfully to one another, there is little hope for creating a more resilient and prosperous society. In this age of growing discord, it is important to acknowledge and respect the wisdom of opinions different from our own. We'd all do well to recognize that diversity of opinion underpins a healthy and vibrant society, just like the diversity of life underpins a vibrant and robust ecosystem. I'd suggest that if you are a climate or environmental-crises skeptic, and you are reading this book, you are doing hugely important work. Well done.

In conclusion, consider the hypothesis that the perception of independence from family, community, or the left or the right is a fallacy. If anything, we are more dependent on others for our survival and well-being than ever before. How many of us grow enough food to support our families? As society becomes more complex, we are more dependent on technology and those who can fix it. We rely on a dizzying array of services including medical help, road building, plumbing, teaching, and so forth. And not only is our dependency on others greater, this dependency has far greater geographical reach than ever before. Many of our products are produced in far-away countries and our purchasing, therefore, has ramifications for people on the other side of the planet. Indeed, our tribe, who actually support our lives, is global. Our urge to connect to our like-minded mini-tribe may feel safe, yet only connecting with like-minded folk is inherently insecure.

### *The Domination of Paid Work*

The third ground-shifting trend, which drives a lot of overconsumption, is a startling trend towards longer work weeks. No longer do we have to hunt and gather our food, nor hand wash our clothes, nor even go to the grocery store in many places. Yet, somehow, in the last few decades, our working hours have been rising. In 2006, the average American single worker worked 180 hours more per year, relative to 1979. That's more than three extra hours a week.[240] The average couple has worked 413 more hours

---

[240] Mishel, L., J. Bernstein, & H. Shierholz 2009, "The state of working America 2008/2009". An Economic Policy Institute book. Ithaca, N.Y., Cornell University Press

per year over this period. That's almost eight hours more a week.[241] Much of this is unpaid overtime, which has risen dramatically in the past decades.

Did you know that it estimated that early hunter gatherers spent 3-4 hours a day working? Ironically, our wealth and timesaving devices facilitate us working more, not spending more time with family, pursuing hobbies, or taking care of ourselves. Longer work hours impact on stress levels, and physical and mental health. And of course, longer paid working hours contribute significantly to unsustainable living practices as we become cash-rich and time-poor. It becomes sensible to buy a new gizmo rather than to try to fix a slightly broken one, to purchase prepared food rather than cook our own.

Tragically, most of us don't even like our paid work. The most extensive study ever on workplace feelings, by Gallup, found that only 13% of the workforce considers work meaningful and looks forward to it. Fully 63% of us are disengaged or sleepwalking through the workday, 24% hate our job.[242] Forty-four percent of Americans say they are often or very often overworked or overwhelmed.[243] Many of my friends complain about being busy and not having enough time to do anything like self-care or have fun. Indeed, a dear friend of mine acknowledged that she hoped her health test results were bad, so she could have a holiday. She is one of the wisest people I know, and such a sentiment really shocked us all, especially her. We can go a long way to fixing these things by removing paid work from the pedestal it occupies. But this will also require an adjustment to our material expectations. Hmm, where have I heard that before?

Lest you think that reducing our material consumption, acknowledging our interdependent and adjusting our work/life balance, lets explore the myriad of ways in which these behavioral changes benefit us.

---

[241] Schor, J.B. 2010, True Wealth, Penguin, New York

[242] Gallup 2013, "State of the Workplace Report", https://www.gallup.com/services/178517/state-global-workplace.aspx

[243] Schor, J.B. 2010, True Wealth, Penguin, New York

# The personal and societal benefits to reducing material consumption, acknowledging interdependent and addressing our work/life balance

## *Changes to Living and Work Patterns*

If we can shift the domination of our time away from our paid work, we give ourselves the opportunity to grow and explore, to play and love, and to contribute to our community. We can do our own work instead, the work of our lives. Perhaps this is to learn yoga, play the piano, raise children, grow flowers, learn a language, grow closer to the divine, love the people in your life, to sew, or to paint. For many of us, working part-time can allow us to do these things as well as to invest in our health and do good for others.

Of course, reducing work hours is not a feasible or appealing solution for everyone. For folks who love their work, more power to them. People who have a calling and can turn it into a job may not want to change their work patterns. However, these folks may have enough wiggle room in their budgets to buy products that support a healthy planet and society. Some people have no option and have to work full-time, and more, simply to feed their families. We'd all like to see that change, I'm sure. But in the consideration of eco-conscious behaviors, the less wealthy amongst us have less of an obligation to address their consumption patterns simply because they don't consume as much and undoubtedly they already practice sustainable habits such as only buying what's really needed, and fixing and borrowing things. So, while this section on changing our work patterns may not apply to everyone, and it may seem onerous to others, it may be more feasible than you'd first think.

Living with less stuff and with less cash is an increasing trend. Books such as True Wealth[244] and Thrive[245] abound,

---

[244] Schor, J.B. 2010, True Wealth, Penguin Books

[245] Huffington, A. 2015, Thrive, Harmony Books

discussing the practicalities and benefits of doing less paid work and how to thrive with less cash. For myself, Your Money or Your Life[246] was paradigm shifting in my relationship with money. This book showed me how I was working so much just to be able to work so much.

This pattern of clinging to the idea that more cash flow improves our lives is repeated at national scales. Our government and industry leaders drone on and on about gross domestic product (GDP) and economic growth. However, while the GDP of the US has risen almost three fold since 1960, the happiness of US citizens has stayed relatively constant. Indeed, there has been a slight downturn in American's happiness in the last few years. The World Happiness Report finds that this recent decline in US happiness is most strongly correlated to the decay of social factors, including reduced social support, freedom to make life choices, as well as increased perceptions of corruption and reduced generosity.[247] Almost all eco-conscious activities can contribute to improving at least one of these social factors. For instance, shopping at the local farmers' market will act to strengthen our community and our sense of freedom and generosity, while increasing our contribution to wealth distribution. For some of us, shifting to part-time work has the potential to be a cornucopia of happiness. I have to note here that nationalized medicine in the UK makes this far easier to achieve. Many of my couple-friends in England both worked part-time when their children were young, so they could each spend more time with the kids. This would more often than not be impossible in the US where health insurance is tied to full time employment.

## *Improved Mental Health*

The modern mental health crisis is rather shocking when we think about the number of people who are affected and how severely they are affected.

---

[246] Robin, V., Dominguez,J. And M. Mustache 2018, Your Money or Your Life, Penguin Books

[247] Helliwell, J. et al 2017 "The World Happiness Report 2017"

- Major depressive episodes are the leading cause of disability and days of lost work in the US.[248]
- 1 in 5 Americans and 1 in 9 Brits take at least one kind of drug for mental health issues.
- Suicide rates tripled for girls aged 10-14, for whom it is a leading cause of death, and increased by almost 50% for men aged 45-65 between 1999 and 2014.[249]

There are nine identified factors which contribute to depression: seven environmental factors and two biological ones. Our lifestyle and work patterns contribute to many of them. The environmental factors which combat depression include: having meaning in our lives, and feeling we have control, that we belong, that we are valued, that we have a secure future, and that we are good at something.[250] These factors can be found at our paid jobs, but apparently not enough as most of us don't like our work. If we can reduce our paid work to pursue things which do satisfy these needs for control, meaning, belonging, and being valued, we'd be much happier. Helping other beings and other humans to have a chance for a vibrant life, by pursuing an eco-conscious life, can give tremendous meaning to our lives. When we live eco-consciously, we are also wrestling back control of our spending patterns. We choose who we support when we know about the products we buy. When we take action to protect the environment and humanity's future, and the world feels less like a whirlwind of chaos. We feel part of something greater than ourselves. We feel better. That is real wealth.

As well as the depression epidemic, there are two other modern conditions that eco-action can help us address: *affluenza* and eco-anxiety. Affluenza is a term coined to describe the anxiety and malaise that the affluent feel because of their economic advantages and, sometimes, the desire for more and more

[248] Mojitabai, R., M. Olfson, B. Han, 2016 "National Trends in the Prevalence and Treatment of Depression in Adolescents and Young Adults" Pediatrics, November 2016

[249] Curtin, S.C., M.Warner and H. Hedegaard 2016, "Increase in Suicide in the United States, 1999-2014", NCHS Data Brief No. 241

[250] Factors contributing to depression

stuff.[251] Affluenza is related to the discomfort we have when we over-consume or when we witness the self-entitlement of others. Excessive materialism makes us feel bloated, spoiled, uncomfortable, and even ill. Eco-anxiety, on the other hand, is a growing sense of worry and panic seen more and more by professionals. Many people are anxious about the decay of our natural resources and don't know what to do about it.

Solutions to all these problems lie within eco-activism. Granted, there are many ways to improve one's mental health, but connecting with nature and other people is seen more and more as a powerful method. Like the experience of a healthy diet, an exercise program, or an alcohol abstinence plan, eco-activism can help us feel better: full of energy, positive and hopeful. When we live eco-consciously, we feel like we are living within our means, being fit, and responsible. Eco-choices give a profound sense of purpose and meaning. And just as with other healthy habits, there's no reason to berate ourselves if we are not doing it perfectly. We start small and see what works for us. Breaking our habit of material consumption, done morally and gracefully, can be a panacea of goodness.

### *Wealth and Power Distribution*

In addition to improving our own happiness, breaking our rampant material consumption and concentrating on local, fair trade, and organic products is also our best tool for addressing the massive wealth and power inequalities in the world. Were you aware that the wealthiest 1% of people in the world have more money than the rest of the people ON THE PLANET? Or that eight men, together, own more than 50% of the population?[252] The income of the top 1% has grown by 300% in the last 30 years, during which time the rise in the income of the US' poorest 50%

---

[251] Affluenza, see https://en.wikipedia.org/wiki/Affluenza Accessed October 11, 2019

[252] Oxfam 2017, "An economy for the 99%", https://www.oxfamamerica.org/explore/research-publications/an-economy-for-the-99-percent/

has been zero, nil, nada, in real money terms.[253] These trends are mainly driven by tax regulations, political lobbying, and business for profit alone -- not for workers', consumers', or ecological well-being. To continue with this inequality saga, if we rank the income stream of companies by sales[254] and governments by revenue,[255] 72 of the 100 biggest economic entities in the world are now corporations, not countries. Together, the world's ten largest companies have revenue greater than 180 countries' governments.[256]

These ultra-wealthy companies include Bank of America (5th), Apple (6th), Royal Dutch Shell (8th), Wells Fargo (10th), Exxon Mobil (11th), AT&T (12th), Samsung (13th), Citigroup (14th), Toyota (15th), Microsoft (16th), Alphabet (17th - parents of Google), Volkswagen (18th), Chevron (19th), and Verizon (20th)[257] where the number in parenthesis gives the company's rank in a merged list of countries and companies revenue. Each of these companies just listed has more revenue than 200 of the 228 countries in the world.[258] These ultra-wealthy companies are primarily businesses in healthcare and insurance, cars and fossil fuels, and computers and phones. And with this wealth, these companies wield

---

[253] UBS/PWC (2016) "Billionaires Insights: Are billionaires feeling the pressure?" http://uhnw-greatwealth.ubs.com/media/8616/billionaires - report - 2016.pdf

[254] Forbes 2019 Ranking of World's Largest Public Companies https://www.forbes.com/global2000/list/2/#header:revenue_sortreverse:true accessed October 10, 2019

[255] Wikipidea "List of Countries by Government Budget" https://en.wikipedia.org/wiki/List_of_countries_by_government_budget accessed October 10, 2019

[256] Oxfam 2017, "An economy for the 99%", https://www.oxfamamerica.org/explore/research-publications/an-economy-for-the-99-percent/

[257] Forbes 2019 Ranking of World's Largest Public Companies https://www.forbes.com/global2000/list/2/#header:revenue_sortreverse:true accessed October 10, 2019

[258] Wikipidea "List of Countries by Government Budget" https://en.wikipedia.org/wiki/List_of_countries_by_government_budget accessed October 10, 2019

outrageous influence on policies, laws, and treaties.[259] Chillingly, research has shown that the percentage of Americans supporting policy has little impact on whether or not a policy is adopted. Contrastingly, when the proportion of large businesses and affluent Americans who support a policy rises, from 0 to 95%, the likelihood that a policy will be adopted rises by 60%.[260] This is either a threat to our democracy or a sign that our democracy has already failed.

Corporations and businesses play prominent roles in encouraging both our individual expectations and societal trends through lobbying, advertising, and campaigning. However, we must remember, we hold the ultimate power through our spending, our voting, and our voices. If we all stopped buying from multinationals, these powers would wilt. And if you feel your dollars won't make a difference, know that they already do make a difference. Though each of our droplets is small, each droplet ripples in a multitude of ways - socially, politically, financially, and environmentally. And the whole is simply the sum of its parts. Even the vast oceans, are only the sum of individual droplets.

## *Strengthened Social Networks and Security*

Our dedication to paid work and our perceived independence contribute to another trend in modern society: the depletion of *social capital*. Social capital is a term coined to bundle together those attributes of human interaction which provide services to people. Social capital thus includes a family providing a financial safety net, neighbors watching out for one another, as well as the business opportunities which social networking can provide. Social capital is the connections among individuals. Harvard professor Robert Putnam, author of the iconic study on social capital, *Bowling Alone*, summarizes that over the 25 years, from 1993 to 2017, Americans have attended 58% fewer club

---

[259] Oxfam 2017, "An economy for the 99%", https://www.oxfamamerica.org/explore/research-publications/an-economy-for-the-99-percent/

[260] Disproportionate representation. Gilens and Page (2014) Gilens, M., & Page, B. (2014). Testing Theories of American Politics: Elites, Interest Groups, and Average Citizens. Perspectives on Politics, 12(3), 564-581. doi:10.1017/S1537592714001595 (see also Oxfam 2017)

meetings, 43% fewer family dinners, and 35% fewer gatherings with friends. This reduction in social engagements has severe impacts on civic, political, economic, and personal well-being as well as contributing to an observed decay of trust in one another.[261]

And if you think that less social interaction is just less fun and games, think again. High social connectivity is linked to better physical and mental health, improved flows of information, money, and moral support, and even the ability to access and respond positively to medical treatments.[262] For example, there is evidence that a robust social network leads to higher rates of recovery from cancer and lower rates of depression if social networks are strong.[263] Increased social capital also strengthens the resilience of businesses. Following Hurricane Katrina, small businesses which had higher levels of connectivity to the community were 21% more likely to be performing at rates greater than their pre-Katrina rates.[264]

In summary, acknowledging our inter-dependence and valuing our social and health capital, at least as much as our financial capital, will contribute to a more resilient community. Eco-conscious choices can improve our life well-being, protect our ecosystems, and redistribute wealth, all while facilitating a more creative, flexible, joy filled life. So by making eco-conscious choices, in addition to enriching your own life through increased connectivity, resilience and health, you are also addressing many of society's more significant injustices. Benefits for you, the environment, and society. What's not to like?

---

[261] http://robertdputnam.com/bowling-alone/social-capital-primer/ accessed March 20, 2019.

[262] Helliwell, J. et al 2017 "The World Happiness Report 2017"

[263] https://en.wikipedia.org/wiki/Social_capital accessed March 26, 2019

[264] Torres, A.P., M.I. Marshall and S. Sydnor, 2018, "Does social capital pay off? The case of business resilience after Hurricane Katrina", Journal of Contingencies and Crisis Management DOI: 10.1111/1468-5973.12248

# 6 UNRAVELING BARRIERS TO ECO-FRIENDLY ACTIONS

Thinking about why we don't engage in eco-friendly activities can help us acknowledge our doubts or shed light on how we've reached our conclusions. Understanding what informs our decisions is especially helpful for decisions made on the go -- such as what to have for dinner or even which appliance to buy. Articulating the reasons why we don't always act in an eco-conscious manner can also help us to be more graceful, to others and ourselves. Of course, at any particular moment or for any specific issue, our knowledge and feelings strongly underpin the choices we make. But there are other factors at play as well. To unpick the potential blocks to eco-actions, it is helpful to array these barriers along a spectrum of increasing belief that environmental action is urgent.

In Figure 6.1 *A Spectrum of Eco-Action Barriers*, I've listed some of the reasons we give for not engaging in eco-conscious choices in a rough order from most restrictive to least. In previous chapters, we've explored some of these barriers and the misconceptions surrounding them. We've discussed some of the reasons for not engaging in eco-friendly activities including 'Distrust', 'Environmentalism=alarmism', 'Special interest', 'Existing mechanisms', 'Not me', and 'Too expensive'. Here, I revisit these and, in addition, discuss a few other hindrances, including 'Green is bad', 'God's plan', and 'I'll do it later' excuses for inaction.

## Distrust

Distrust is the most difficult eco-action barrier to overcome and also the one with the most disbelief that eco-action is urgent. It is exceedingly difficult, if not impossible, to have productive discourse if everything is doubted or discarded. It is impossible to prove that you are not all figments of my imagination, after all. :^) I discussed this trust issue at length in Chapter 1. I think it is a great sorrow of our modern culture and perhaps the greatest hindrance to protecting our natural resources.

I experienced this very personally and was profoundly upset when I realised that climate change scientists are distrusted and doubted. Out of a sense of morality, I left a field I loved in order to work on environmental issues and spent, and continue to spend, much of my spare time on activism aiming to help other critters and people. I felt affronted, and offended, to learn that some people think climate scientists value money or fame over truth. Most people who succeed in academia work could have used their dedication and brains to pursue careers that brought wealth rather than knowledge. What's more, science is all about uncovering nature's truths. That's its whole aim. And in the extremely competitive world of science, anyone who lies or fabricates will be unflinchingly cut down. Of course, there are instances of researchers who have been dishonest, but I've never personally known of a case in the over 30 years I've been working in the field of science.

Isn't it more likely that those who benefit from depleting our natural resources are lying to us? For instance, oil companies have far more to lose than scientists have to gain by a reduction in fossil fuel use. We now know that Exxon was aware of the possibility of climate change as early as the 1970s, and aggressively funded climate denial research and misinformation organizations.[265] For sure, Exxon had billions of dollars at stake. On the other hand, climate scientists are highly trained individuals who could work in other fields. Researchers will not starve if the climate science budget shrinks.

If you find that you doubt scientific statements, I encourage you to try to unpick that reaction. If your distrust stems from a religious conviction, remember that science is simply a tool to try to understand the natural world and can not address our deepest spiritual beliefs. Yes, it may change our understanding of the

---

[265] Wikipedia, ExxonMobil climate change controversy, accessed September 11, 2020, https://en.wikipedia.org/wiki/ExxonMobil_climate_change_controversy

world, "The world is round", "The earth moves around the sun", but it can not address the fundamental question of whether or not God exists. Science and religion are not fundamentally at odds with one another. Rather, they are two, potentially supporting, lenses through which to interpret our observations of the world.

Encouragingly, it seems that society is beginning to recognize this problem of distrust, both of experts and of our neighbors. Acknowledgement of this trust deficit will help us to build a more cohesive, nurturing and productive society. As noted in the introductory chapter, key ways to help us rebuild our trust of one another are to acknowledge our common goals and to respect people whose opinions differ from our own.

## Environmentalism = Alarmism

The perception that environmentalists are alarmists is closely related to the lack of trust issue. There are undoubtedly examples of exaggeration, but these have not held up under the rigors of scientific scrutiny. This is how we know they were exaggerations. To combat the exaggeration accusation, the facts presented in Figure 2.1 *The Planetary Wheel,* are mostly taken from large scale reviews of the existing literature. These are studies which review hundreds if not thousands of peer reviewed papers such that numbers and quantities presented have been tested from different angles and very rigorously demonstrated.

If you know any scientists, you know we like nothing better than to say someone else is wrong. Mistakes, misguidance, and deceit are highly unlikely to last in the scientific literature. Unless you think the scientific world is all one great conspiracy, then it makes sense to discard the alarmist viewpoint. If you hold to the alarmist viewpoint or distrust science in general, then it is consistent to also give up flying, the internet, and going to the doctor.

A quick look at the state of the 8 natural resources shows that we've depleted 50% or more of many of our resources. We are operating outside of safe boundaries. As a result, ecosystems are suffering, and some have collapsed. Fish, bird, and mammal populations have all been severely depleted. Insect numbers are frighteningly low compared to 50 years ago. Aside from destroying other species and harming less wealthy folk, the very existence of humanity is actually under threat. How will fruit be pollinated if the insect trend of the last 50 years is continued and we are left with ZERO insects? Based on recent trends this would take about 75 more years of pesticides, habitat destruction, and climate change. And it is not just fruit and veg that we'd lose, for insects also turn over nutrients. This is a polite way of saying bugs eat the dead and feces and make their nutrients available for the next generation. Not to mention that insects are essential to the terrestrial food chain.

And it is not just scientists who are worried. There are countless international treaties, conventions, laws, banks, governments, and businesses which acknowledge the need for a dramatic change in how we treat the natural world. These groups warn that without large-scale change there will be dramatically more famine, drought, flooding, and fires. It is not alarmist to be worried about these impacts.

## Green is bad

Sometimes I hear the opinion that green solutions are bad for the economy and one's pocketbook while being insensitive to job losses. As far as green being economically damaging, extensive research has shown that this is patently untrue. To quote the United Nations' Green Economy Report, "Mounting evidence also suggests that transitioning to a green economy has sound economic and social justification."[266] The transition to a green economy can result in short-term losses of jobs over the first four years, but job gains exceed the losses after four years. An illustrative example is fisheries. Currently, 52% of commercial fish stocks are fully exploited with a further 28% overexploited or depleted. Left unchecked, this will lead to the permanent collapse of many fish stocks and thus huge numbers of job losses. Green fishing practices will mean the fish stocks will thrive. Thus, although there may be temporary job losses, in the long-term,

---

[266] UNEP 2011, "Towards a Green Economy: Pathways to Sustainable Development and Poverty Eradication - A Synthesis for Policy Makers", www.unep.org/greeneconomy

fishing jobs will be secured, as opposed to wiped out. This benefit of tightening our belts for several years will reap long-term economic benefits across many sectors. Poignantly, COVID green economy recovery packages are expected to create more jobs, provide higher returns and lead to greater long term savings than conventional spending packages, in the short term as well as the long term.[267]

The UN's Green Economy Report shows that a global transition to a green economy could be kickstarted by an investment of 2% of GDP per year. This is comparable to the cost of current subsidies to fossil fuels. This 2% of GDP also represents only 10% of annual global investment. So while 2% is not insignificant, it is not insurmountable by any stretch, and given the existential risks seems like a no-brainer. And this is even before we consider that a transition to a green economy is predicted to reduce poverty. After five years, a green economy is also predicted to increase global GDP alongside the above noted net gain in jobs.[268]

Investment in a green economy seems like an obvious best move to make. What makes it difficult for America to adopt these strategies is that big oil, big pharma and big agriculture have a disproportionate influence on our senators and representatives. A recent study showed that the number of individual Americans who support a US policy has no influence on whether or not it is adopted. Disturbingly, it is how many economic elites or business-owned interest groups supported a policy that had a strong influence on adoption. Sometimes I wonder if electoral finance reform is not the biggest single issue of our times.[269] Nonetheless, the green economy is gaining traction. Green economics is mentioned more frequently in speeches and documents from heads of state, finance ministers, and G20 communiques. This is

---

[267] Harvey, F. May 5, 2020, The Guardian, "Green stimulus can repair global economy and climate, says study says"

[268] UNEP 2011, "Towards a Green Economy: Pathways to Sustainable Development and Poverty Eradication - A Synthesis for Policy Makers", www.unep.org/greeneconomy

[269] Gilens, M. and B.I. Page 2014, "Testing Theories of American Politics: Elites, Interest Groups, and Average Citizens", Perspectives on Politics 12 p. 564

another instance of why our actions are so critical. Our choices send financial and societal signals to our political leaders about whether or not to address natural resource depletion.

The second strand of 'green is bad' is the perception that the green agenda is pro-environment but anti-people. This is misrepresentative, as hopefully the preceding paragraphs have shown. Nonetheless, let's explore the underlying principles of environmental groups. UNEP, the United Nations Environment Program, defines a green economy as one that "results in improved human wellbeing and social equity, while significantly reducing environmental risks and ecological scarcities."[270] The 10 key values of the Green Party include only two of which could be construed as primarily environmentally-oriented: ecological wisdom and future thinking. The other eight principles of the Green Party are primarily social values including decentralization of power, grassroots democracy, social justice, nonviolence, community-based economics, feminism, respect for diversity, and personal and global responsibility.[271] You might not agree with all those ideals, but you can hardly claim that it is anti-people.

And don't forget, healthy ecosystems are essential for human survival. UNEP's Green Economy Report summarizes "... the greening of economies is not generally a drag on growth but rather a new engine of growth; that it is a net generator of decent jobs, and that it is also a vital strategy for the elimination of persistent poverty."[272]

## Special Interest

With half of many of our 8 essential natural resources already gone, or in a bad state, the very existence of humanity is under threat. We are already very negatively affected by natural

[270] UNEP 2011, "Towards a Green Economy: Pathways to Sustainable Development and Poverty Eradication - A Synthesis for Policy Makers", www.unep.org/greeneconomy

[271] https://www.greenparty.org/values.php accessed February 28, 2018

[272] UNEP 2011, "Towards a Green Economy: Pathways to Sustainable Development and Poverty Eradication - A Synthesis for Policy Makers", www.unep.org/greeneconomy

system changes, including losses of soil, polluted oceans, dirty air, insufficient freshwater, toxic pollutants, and shifting climates with its bouquet of intensifying hurricanes, high sea levels, flooding, crop failures, droughts, wildfires, and so on. This depletion of roughly 50% occurred primarily over the last 50 years, give or take. Therefore, consumption at current rates and with the current population will lead to the collapse of many of these 8 Resources in the next 50 years or so. And of course population and per capita consumption are growing. The loss of any one of our 8 Natural Resources may well lead to the end of civilization as we know it, massive loss of life, and perhaps even human extinction. A greener society is, therefore, fundamentally essential for human survival.

There are more reasons why eco-choices are not special interests. Eco-conscious consumer choices can also address issues of social justice, wealth inequality, and physical and mental well-being, as outlined in the previous chapter. Indeed, the UN Sustainable Development Goals Report concludes that relief from poverty is inextricably linked to clean water, clean air, healthy land and ocean ecosystems, and a stable climate.[273] In low-income countries, ecosystem services directly underpin livelihoods and form a safety net against natural disasters and economic shocks.[274] Environmentalism is, in fact, the exact opposite of a special interest. Having a robust, vibrant, biodiverse planet is of general interest economically and socially as well as biologically.

## God's plan

A further reason people give for not being engaged in eco-conscious living is that what is happening in the world is all part of God's plan. We can not change things, all is on course, so concentrate on your relationship with God. I've never understood how one's relationship with God could be alright if you are ignoring

---

273 UN 2017, Sustainable Development Goals Report, https://www.un.org/development/desa/publications/sdg-report-2017.html

274 UNEP 2011, "Towards a Green Economy: Pathways to Sustainable Development and Poverty Eradication - A Synthesis for Policy Makers", www.unep.org/greeneconomy

the destruction of the magnificence of creation. Shouldn't we be caring for and nurturing the beautiful things God has created? Even if we are in the end times, we should still be fighting the good fight. When we ignore the environmental devastation that arises from our consumption, we become complicit in the natural world's destruction. That can not be right. In addition to creation's inherent value, the beauty of nature brings many people spiritual awakenings. This is certainly true for me. Being outside and noticing the progression of daffodils, the call of a blue jay, or the touch of a refreshing breeze makes me feel more connected to the divine.

The practices of many faiths and sustainability are very closely aligned. When I married my husband, I was overwhelmed by the dedication and moral strength of his profoundly Christian family. Their faith led me to study the Bible for a couple of years. The central message I found was to give away as much as I could and give till it hurt. Everyone has their own interpretation of the Bible of course. Still, the theme of loving one's neighbor and giving to them freely is, as I understand it, central to Christianity. Interestingly enough, 25 years later, I've circled back around to this belief that sharing our wealth effusively is central to solving our environmental problems. I've also come to a rudimentary understanding that our accumulated financial wealth often acts as a spiritual barrier, eye of the needle and all. I found these truths by wanting to protect the natural world rather than through a biblical study, but the two vantage points certainly align.

It has happened to me time and again that my drive to protect nature mirrors biblical lessons. Another striking example occurred when Alan, a dear friend of mine, spoke to his Rabbi about my vegetarianism. The Rabbi had suggested that vegetarianism is an instinctual way of living a kosher life. Alan and I were able to share food more graciously after that. Rather than being anti-religious, I believe my environmental activism stems from a deep spiritual motivation: a respect for other life, be they humans today or tomorrow or other species. In particular, I believe the message of this book -- reducing consumption and increasing community -- is in line with Christianity on so many fronts.

It saddens me that Christianity and environmentalism are so often seen to conflict. I see this division as having arisen from

# *Figure 6.1. Eco-Action Barriers*

Distrust: Disbelief of those who say there is a problem. *To combat the growing social divide, we need to respect that others have their own wisdom & that scientists are not trying to trick humanity.*

Environmentalist = Alarmist: Eco-worries are exaggerated. *Unfortunately, we are actually facing a multitude of existential threats from environmental pollution and depletion.*

Green is bad: Green choices lead to job losses. *In five years plus, an eco-economy leads to more jobs. A COVID green stimulus package leads to more jobs now, greater returns & long term savings.*

Special interest issue: Environmentalism is for hippies and is unsympathetic to people. *Green values are intimately tied to social & intergenerational justice as well as diversifying our wealth & resiliency.*

God's plan: God's will be done. *We are not meant to give up the good fight just because an outcome may be pre-ordained. Nor should we be party to destroying creation.*

Existing mechanisms: Technology, the economy or the government will solve our environmental problems. *Technology, economics, treaties, and policies have all been trying to address natural resource depletion for years & have not succeeded.*

I'll do it later: Yes, environmental issues are important, but we have to sort out (insert problem) first. *There will always be other pressing issues to resolve, but we are running out of time to save species, ecosystems and possibly the future of humanity.*

Not me: I can't make an impact and I'm not responsible anyway. *Each of us makes far ranging impacts already, and, of course we are responsible for the kind of impact we are making.*

Too expensive: I don't have enough time or the money. *Sometimes, eco-behavior costs more time and money, but often not. Furthermore, the gains in mental and physical health, community building and security, etc, usually dwarf the economic costs.*

media, politicians, or others, trying to ring-fence their supporters to ensure their loyalty. However it has developed, the perceived chasm between environmentalists and some conservative Christians is a false divide. Hearteningly, there are more and more Christian environmental movements that aim to heal this wound.

## Existing mechanisms

A different sort of barrier is the belief that while something ought to be done about environmental issues, it is not for individuals to sort out the mess. Instead, some believe societal mechanisms are the best way to address our environmental problems. While economy, technology, and policy are critical levers, leaving the salvation of nature to these mechanisms will never work. First of all, these mechanisms only change when there are ample financial and social incentives to change. And secondly, while there have been advances in technology and laws, ecological destruction is still ongoing, widespread, and increasing. Existing mechanisms have had ample opportunity to stop or slow the loss of our resources. But they have failed to do so. As our natural capital continues to be depleted, we need to acknowledge that large-scale societal structures are not sufficient to stop the ongoing devastation. I could simply end this section right here. 'The proof is in the pudding' as they say. But I shall elaborate on some of the recent discussions around why technological, market, and governmental fixes to our environmental crises are failing.

### *Existing Mechanism: Technological Fixes*

Some folks believe that improvements in efficiency will reduce our resource usage. A recent broad-ranging analysis of 57 products, ranging from aluminum to transistors, showed that despite technological improvements, overall resource usage increased. Even in cases where there have been dramatic reductions in the amount of material needed to make a product, there has been an even greater increase in demand. A stark example is the use of silicon in mobile phones. Despite significant decreases in the amount of silicon used to build one mobile phone, the number of phones sold has skyrocketed such that the overall global consumption of silicon has increased by 345% in the last four decades.[275] Increased efficiency leading to greater consumption and resulting in more resource use, is known as the rebound effect. It is generally attributed to price drops accompanying the increased efficiency in the product, and thus higher consumer demand. The authors of the 57-products study carried out a further investigation to look for cases where resource use actually declined. They found only six products whose usage had declined, including five which were toxic materials whose use was restricted by governments.[276]

It is not just this one study that has documented the rebound effect. An English economist, W.S. Jevons, observed in 1865 that improvements in coal burning resulted in more coal being burnt. He argued, over 150 years ago, that increased efficiency could not be relied on to reduce consumption.[277] He has been proven to have been prescient. Advances in technology are not reducing resource. While technological innovations have poured forth in the last 150 years, our resource consumption is still increasing, both per-capita and overall. Resource consumption per capita increased by about 28%, in the recent decade between 2000 to 2010.[278]

## *Existing Mechanisms: Market Fixes*

In addition to relying on the efficacy of technological fixes to solve resource depletion, some hold that the market will sort out resource depletion. I have a deep distrust of relying on the economy to protect the environment and the future of humanity. In the first instance, strict capitalism fails to recognize the value in either natural capital or social justice. Indeed both are referred to as *externalities* in mainstream economics. That nomenclature

---

[275] Magee, C. & T.C. Devezas 2017, "A simple extension of dematerialization theory: Incorporation of technical progress and the rebound effect", Technological Forecasting & Social Change 117, 196

[276] https://news.mit.edu/2017/technological-progress-alone-stem-consumption-materials-0119 accessed October 16, 2019

[277] https://en.wikipedia.org/wiki/Jevons_paradox, accessed October 16, 2019

[278] West, J. et al 2016, UNEP: Global Material Flows and Resource Productivity. Paris, United Nations Environment Programme.

alone is dismissive. As consumers, we have become blinded by the bottom line, and this in turn, drives manufacturers to concentrate on producing less expensive products. For an individual company in a competitive market, it can cost much less to dump hazardous materials than to rethink how a product is made. There are, of course, countless other examples of bottom line reasoning winning out. The company's directors are between a rock and a hard place - pollution or bankruptcy. As the Nobel Peace Prize winner for alleviating poverty, Muhammad Yumus, argues, unfettered capitalism inevitably leads to rampant inequality, unemployment, and environmental destruction.[279]

And it isn't just a handful of economists who are recognizing the failure of the marketplace to protect the environment. Mainstream economics is now exploring alternatives to the standard economic model to understand how we can protect our natural resources. One alternative is full economic costing, whereby a product's cost includes the product's entire life cycle in the price tag, from production, through usage, to disposal. This idea has the advantage that it incentivizes industry to find less damaging alternatives. As polluting-product-costs skyrocket, consumers would likely choose the environmentally friendly options. It seems only right that the cost of a product should include its clean-up or disposal. Clean-up and disposal are part of running a house, why shouldn't they be part of the economy?

Of course, there are difficulties in enacting full-economic-costings. It is problematic to calculate the cost of clean-up and disposal of any given product. Nonetheless, there are efforts to do so. Notably, The Economics of Ecosystems and Biodiversity initiative estimates the annual economic values of forests, per acre:

- $560 for timber,
- $61 for fuel wood,
- $41-70 non-timber forest products,
- $842-2265 for climate regulation,
- $24 for flood regulation,
- $51 for pollination services, and

---

[279] http://muhammadyunus.org/index.php/yunus-centre/2015-04-26-06-56-02/books accessed February 28, 2018

- $46 for humanity's desire to have forests.

These numbers demonstrate that a single acre of forest can provide $1,625-$3,077 of services every year. In contrast, harvesting it only yields $560 worth of timber. Such an approach has helped to reduce deforestation in Mexico by almost ⅓ and to prevent the draining of a water purifying swamp next to Kampala, Uganda.[280]

There is a moral push back against this commodification of nature - how can we put a price tag on life itself? Some counter this argument with the observations that we already price nature but do so unconsciously, with the result being a very low price for natural resources. Pricing nature also leads to such practices as exchanging one forest for another or even building a replacement woodland if another is destroyed. A little thought will remind us that a new forest will not have the resilience nor the diversity which a 5,000-year-old ecosystem will have.

Two other aspects of standard market fixes which are problematic are the calls for economic growth and subsidies. Many economists now recognize that to have a healthy economy; it must either stop growing or grow in a very different way.[281] Resource usage can not continue to grow. Indeed it must be reduced. If we insist on the economic growth model, the focus must shift away from manufactured products to low impact, arguably high quality, products, services, creative pursuits, and so forth. As noted above, over a five-year time scale, a green economy is expected to yield a growing economy in terms of jobs, wealth creation, and the GDP.[282]

Some economists go even further and argue that the growth model itself is flawed. They suggest that instead of judging our governments in terms of GDP, perhaps we should value how

---

[280] TEEB 2010, The Economics of Ecosystems and Biodiversity: Mainstreaming the Economics of Nature: A synthesis of the approach, conclusions and recommendations of TEEB

[281] Howarth, R.A. 2012, "Sustainability, wellbeing and Economic Growth", *Minding Nature* 5.2, p32, https://www.humansandnature.org/sustainability-wellbeing-and-economic-growth accessed Oct 24, 2019

[282] UNEP 2011, "Towards a Green Economy: Pathways to Sustainable Development and Poverty Eradication - A Synthesis for Policy Makers", www.unep.org/greeneconomy

much our social structures improve the wellbeing of our citizens.[283] Seen in this light, the business-as-usual economic model fares very poorly as it is leading to shortages of our life sustaining resources.

And as for subsidies, a recent report estimated that global fossil fuel subsidies made up 6.5% of the global domestic product in 2015 (led by China, the US, Russia, Europe, and India). The same study estimated that stopping global fossil fuel subsidies would reduce carbon emissions by 21% and the annual 3.5 million deaths from air pollution by 55%.[284] A summit of G7 countries, another of G20 nations, as well as the World Bank and the International Energy Agency have all concluded that cutting fossil fuel subsidies is the single greatest policy step to combat global warming and the wasteful use of energy.

*Existing Mechanisms: Government and Policy Fixes*

In addition to economical and technological solutions, some folks think the government will or should fix our environmental problems. There are numerous international agreements to limit biodiversity loss, to reduce carbon emissions, and so forth. But again, we continue to use our natural resources at a pace faster than the earth systems can replace them. I would also argue that it is not the place of the government to set social trends, instead, leaders should be the personification of societal values. We can not look to the government, technology, or the economy to swoop in and solve our problems. Rather we must demonstrate to these large scale actors, through our spending and voting, what our values are. It is our practices and spending patterns that drive our society forwards.

## I'll do it later

*Later* is a tricky barrier, but one which I hear a lot. It needs to be faced by those who believe environmental issues are a

---

283 Helliwell, J., R. Layard, J. Sachs et al 2017, World Happiness Report, https://worldhappiness.report/

284 Coady, D., I. Parry, L. Sears and B. Shang 2017, "How large are global fossil fuel subsidies?" World Development 91, 11-27.

problem, but that now is not the time. This line of reasoning may argue that there are other more pressing issues that we must deal with first. There are two reasons why this is fatal thinking. First of all, all political problems are also inherently environmental ones. Consider Brexit or the US-Mexico wall. How will the UK establish environmental regulations post Brexit? And why have 28 wildlife protection laws been waived to build the US-Mexico wall? There is an internationally important wildlife refuge along the path of the wall which will be largely destroyed.[285] At this time, or more poignantly, at this state of natural resource depletion, our decisions need to consider the consequent impacts on the natural world. The point is not that we should consider *only* the environment, but that the environment must be a consideration in our choices.

The second reason putting off environmental action is a bad idea is that we do not know exactly where breaking points are in ecological systems. The drastically depleted status of our natural resources now, suggests that the time for easy action was yesterday. A little more depletion may see collapses of natural cycles. Will a loss of 60% of coral reefs result in the collapse of some commercial fisheries? Or is the threshold of catastrophic collapse 70%? 80%?

In the case of greenhouse gas emissions, the Nobel Prize winning Intergovernmental Panel on Climate Change has made an estimate of the threshold to avoid catastrophic results. The Panel warns that we need to avoid global temperatures rising by more than 1.5°C / 2.7F. This would require that we reduce greenhouse gas emissions by 45% by 2030 and that we become carbon neutral by 2050. If we do not, we *dramatically* increase the risk of fires, drought, flooding, extreme heat, and poverty for hundreds of millions of people. Part of the reason the risks increase so dramatically beyond 1.5°C, is that beyond this threshold there is a far greater chance that some natural systems will switch from being carbon sinks to being carbon sources. So instead of the soil absorbing ¼ of the carbon we emit, it may become a source. Furthermore, permafrost may start melting

---

[285] https://www.npr.org/2018/11/01/660671247/butterfly-preserve-on-the-border-threatened-by-trumps-wall accessed October 24, 2019

beyond 1.5°C and release huge quantities of carbon into the atmosphere. Exceeding 1.5°C could lead to further heating, more carbon release, more heating, in an escalating feedback. Even the more moderate aim of limiting the global temperature rise to 2°C, requires a reduction in emissions of 25% by 2030 and carbon neutrality by 2070. While there is undoubtedly some flexibility here in terms of the exact timing, there ***is*** an overwhelming scientific consensus that 2030, give or take a year or two, is an important timespan in which to get carbon emissions down by a hard minimum of 25%. And that we need to be carbon neutral by 2050 or we will suffer tragic impacts.[286] Our emissions are currently *growing*, with the most recent data I could find indicating that our emissions increased by 1.3% in 2017.[287] This urgency for significantly reducing emissions has been reported on by a broad range of new agencies, including Fox news.[288] I wonder, has the need for carbon emission reductions stuck in your mind? Will it now?

## Not me

As to the barrier that 'I'm not responsible' or 'I can't make an impact', we'd all do well to remember that you can't make an ocean without droplets. The content of each of our droplets makes a difference and we are each responsible for those contents. Many people also consider it a moral obligation to live with others in mind. What's more, only if we live with others in mind will society, manufacturing and governance evolve to reflect these values. Another point to remember is that, our actions influence people around us. We will probably never know the full impact of our actions, but your actions may be the catalyst which changes

---

286 IPCC 2018, Special Report: Global Warming of 1.5oC, Summary for Policy Makers https://www.ipcc.ch/sr15/chapter/summary-for-policy-makers/ accessed April 4, 2019

287 Oliver, J.G.J. and J.A.H.W. Peteres, 2018 "Trends in global $CO_2$ and greenhouse gas emissions" PBL Netherlands Environmental Assessment Agency

288 https://www.foxnews.com/science/terrifying-climate-change-warning-12-years-until-were-doomed accessed April 3, 2019

millions of people's behavior or even prevents a war. On the other hand, if we don't act responsibly, we have to own responsibility for negative consequences. While social structures undoubtedly need to change too, it is individuals who can change right now.

## It's too expensive

The last item on the spectrum of eco-action-barriers is the 'It's too expensive, financially or time-wise"' excuse. This is undoubtedly my greatest obstacle to action. Of course this is an insurmountable obstacle to many for certain eco-actions. And on the other hand, there are many cases where sustainable options are less expensive. But for those times when eco-options are more expensive, we can still get caught up in society's rhetoric that we should aim to save money. Sometimes I feel guilty because my food bills are pretty high and I vow to be less indulgent. But, when I think about it rationally, my food bills are high because organic products often cost more, sometimes even local produce costs more. So, it helps me to remember that the organic broccoli I'm buying is not poisoning the insects and our waterways, my local apple is supporting neighboring farmers, and I am helping wealth equality. Furthermore, the local and/or organic products taste better and have more nutrients. I'm not really buying the same product. Then it doesn't seem expensive to me. I find that saying to myself *"I'm voting with my money"* is a shorthand phrase that reminds me that eco-friendly options are in line with my values.

## What's left?

What is left if the economy, technology, and the government are failing to protect the environment? After decades of thinking about these issues, I have concluded that the key lever is how we, as individuals, spend our money. Every purchase we make sends a myriad of signals. Not only do our choices influence business and government spheres, but our decisions also affect ourselves, our family, friends, and community. In turn, how our community behaves is possibly the most influential lever in how we behave, thus extending the influence of our personal eco-choices. While we may tend to blame multinationals for our environmental ills, those multinationals only exist because we have financially supported them. Capitalists are only doing what capitalism asks of them - making decisions that optimize profits for the shareholders, company owners, or themselves. Who is to blame? Me? The board member? The government? All of us? Probably. But more poignantly, who can change right now? I can. You can.

I think this message that we need to reduce our consumption has been the elephant in the room for far too long. Many environmentalists and politicians appear to avoid talking about reducing consumption, perhaps because they believe it will make them unpopular. Don't drive. Don't eat meat. Don't buy that new phone. From the individual to national economies, we are encouraged to think that more consumption is good, lower prices, and more money in our pockets are positives. But, quite simply, this isn't the case. Once we have met our basic needs, it has been shown over and over that more stuff and more money do not make us happier.[289] I think most of us know this. I believe many of us who have more wealth than we need for basic survival, live with a general feeling of unease. Many in the middle class have an unstated anxiety about being over indulgent, over privileged, and bloated. What is your reaction to the shopping frenzy at Christmas time? What do you think about how much stuff kids, or adults, have? Monetary overindulgence is much like overeating, creating a cycle of unhealthy spending, binge budgets, and guilt. As noted above, the accompanying feelings of malaise, guilt and isolation have been named Affluenza.

How do we cure ourselves of Affluenza? Not to be offhanded, or diminishing how hard it can be to fight these kinds of malaises, but doing things for others is always a good source of purpose and connectivity. And in this particular case, the solution is in the disease. If we feel a lack of motivation - let the crises of the world's poor and the state of the natural world motivate us. If we feel guilty about having too much, we can share our wealth

---

[289] Kahneman, D. and A. Deaton 2010, "High income improves evaluation of life but not emotional wellbeing", PNAS 107, 16489

and focus less on accumulating money and stuff. And if we feel isolated, we can try getting stuck into our community. I believe that protecting wilderness and people is the grand fight of our generation. But how do we go about instilling a sense of motivation and connecting to our community?

Many in the eco-movement have long believed that education will change people's behavior towards green choices. Not only has this argument been weakened by research,[290] but it is also rather condescending and self defeating. While education and knowledge are, of course, important parts of living moral lives, there must be an exchange of ideas rather than a lecture of 'I / We know best.' Strengthening our community, and being kind and respectful of people who hold different opinions than we do, is the first step in influencing anyone. Then, by drawing on the wisdom of all actors, we can find solutions together. I hope that this book helps us to acknowledge some common ground, perhaps one of these: *all people are created equal, future generations deserve a chance to live, wilderness is sacred.* All three of these lead to the necessity to protect our natural resources.

Instead of policy, economics, or technological fixes, which are all failing to slow resource depletion, we could consider a completely different tact. E.O. Wilson, a highly respected biologist, suggested that we set aside 50% of the planet for wilderness.[291] If we do set aside half the planet in this way, it is not that we couldn't interact with it, or indeed let indigenous peoples live in their ancestral homes. We would just consider the health of ecosystems as paramount in these areas. In 2010, 196 parties to the Convention on Biological Diversity, that is, all UN countries, except the United States, became legally bound to protect 17% of the Earth's land surface and 10% of the world's oceans. These are the so-called Aichi targets.[292] As of 2018, 15% of global land and

---

[290] Peattie, K. 2010, "Green consumption: behavior and norms", Ann. Rev. Environ. Resour. 35: 195-228 and Chapter 4.

[291] E.O. Wilson 2016, *Half-Earth, Our Planet's Fight for Life*, Liveright Publishing, New York

[292] https://en.wikipedia.org/wiki/Convention_on_Biological_Diversity accessed October 24, 2019

7% of the global ocean areas are protected.[293] That's a good start. And it's not too difficult to increase that. For instance, if we reduced our meat consumption to recommended levels, and protected the 1.6 billion acres thus freed up, we'd have nearly 20% of the land surface protected. If we all became vegetarian and protected all the land thus freed up from agriculture,nearly 40% of global land area could be protected.[294] Perhaps we should consider compromising: reducing meat consumption and aiming for 30% of the global land surface protected, for example

For myself, writing this book, and further educating myself, has made a difference. Writing about meat's impact, for instance, has made me step-up my eco-conscious eating. I've been a naughty vegetarian for 30 years, not eating mammals but occasionally eating foul and fish. I've had the determination to reduce my consumption of these this past year. It feels good. I'm hoping to concentrate next year on exploring more vegan meals, growing more of my own food, and further reducing my food waste, food miles, and processed foods. But even more urgent to my mind, is engaging in more conversations with differently minded folk.

The discussion of these barriers to action reminds me that there are many snags to prevent environmental engagement. And while this multi-snag observation may be daunting, it is also a positive message about individual action. For when we flip the multi-snag snare around, we find that each and every one of our eco-conscious activities makes small, but profound, tears all along the spectrum of barriers. Perhaps your dent will be the one to crumble a wall.

---

293 McKie, R. Feb 17, 2018, "Should we give up half of the Earth to wildlife?", The Guardian, https://www.theguardian.com/environment/2018/feb/18/should-we-give-half-planet-earth-wildlife-nature-reserve

294 World Wildlife Fund 2017, Appetite for Destruction

# 7 Reasons for Hope

Many people tell me that they are very depressed and anxious about the state of the natural world. I get that. Things are pretty dire. If we don't change our consumption patterns, lots of people today and into the future will suffer greatly. Ecosystems are fragmented, as well as subjected to a brutal cocktail of stresses. Wildlife populations are showing disturbing signs of trouble. Humanity as a whole may be responsible for a great mass extinction. What a legacy for our generation. I've worried about this for decades. But oddly enough, I feel more hopeful now than ever before. And that is primarily because the acknowledgement of the seriousness of environmental catastrophes is becoming mainstream. It is creeping into our collective awareness. I'd always hoped that we'd start dealing with our careless practices before we reached the crisis point. But part of me thought it likely that for the majority to take note would require dire circumstances. And while we do have a frightening depletion of natural resources, humanity is taking note. And that's a huge relief.

More and more people are coming to appreciate that nature is an essential common good. We are recognizing that we can and that we need to come together to preserve the environment. We are starting to understand that our activities have led to the loss of 50% of insects and vertebrates. There are daily news stories about plastics, pollution, and inhumane working conditions, as well as countless conversations about eco-issues. There are local initiatives and non-profit organizations as well as state, national, and international efforts to protect nature. Technological advances continue. There are numerous eco-friendly trends like living simply, tiny houses, organic foods, slow food, vegetarianism and veganism, and supporting local businesses. It all just needs notching up another step. If we could get in the mode we were in during World War II, I've no doubt we could build an equitable and nurturing modern society that is both comfy and secure. While it is frightening that we've now arrived at the point where eco-problems threaten our very existence, be assured that we have the knowledge, the grit, and the resources to thrive and nurture.

We can also take heart from the strength of nature itself, which has rebounded from disasters, decimation, and toxic pollutants to become vibrant and diverse again. Looking forward, we see that there are many excellent solutions at our fingertips. While looking back, we can celebrate many eco-success stories. In this chapter, we explore past and ongoing successful campaigns as well as examples of work and research that aim to solve large and small issues. And perhaps most critically, is the fact that eco-awareness is growing. Acceptance of our responsibility to protect natural resources is the keystone which will transform our perception of eco-consciousness from a niggling burden to essential work and opportunities.

## Success stories

We can look to the recent past to be reminded that we can and have won environmental battles.

### *Reducing Acid Rain.*

In the 1970s, acid rain became a household name. We learned that sulphuric acid in rain was defoliating forests in Europe, polluting rivers, and corroding man-made structures. Acid rain forms when particular industrial and fossil fuel emissions mix with rainwater. Legislation was fought for and finally put in place. It has recently been estimated that consequent reductions in sulfur emissions in the EU have prevented 80,000 premature human deaths every year.[295]

### *Repairing the Ozone Hole.*

A similar success story is the reduction in the atmospheric ozone hole. The ozone hole is a thinning of an atmospheric layer of ozone which absorbs ultraviolet radiation from the sun. Without the ozone layer, ultraviolet radiation would reach the earth's

---

[295] Turnock, S.T. et al 2016, " The impact of European legislative and technology measures to reduce air pollutants on air quality, human health and climate", Environ. Res. Lett. **11** 024010

surface and can cause cancer. The International Montreal Protocol regulated the emissions of ozone destroying compounds leading to the reversal of ozone layer thinning and a continued recovery towards pre-industrial ozone quantities in the atmosphere. The Montreal protocol is often referred to as one of the greatest environmental success stories in history.[296]

*Reforestation.*

There are many reforestation success stories around the globe. In my homeland, New England, forests covered 90% of the land prior to the settlement of Europeans. However coverage was reduced to just 20% in the 1800s. A relatively recent commitment to sustainable harvesting practices by private landowners and conservation groups has meant that New England's forests are now gaining ground. Forest cover in Massachusetts, for example, is back up to 60%.[297]

## People are amazing

There are many examples of individuals making a significant impact on environmental systems. Jane Goodall, who is my lifelong hero, has combined excellent science with reforesting and conservation successes. She has helped us understand that other animals use tools and how complex chimpanzee society is. And if that were not enough, her story demonstrates how kindness and moms can make all the difference. I heard Dr. Goodall speak many years ago and she told the story of how her mom made all of Dr. Goodall's subsequent work possible. The local Tanzanians were uncomfortable with a young woman being on her own in the forest, so Dame Goodall's mom went with her to Tanzania. Dr. Goodall's mom subsequently became the go-to person in the area for medical help as she had a lot of medical knowledge and was happy to be of use. This fostered trust between the Goodalls and the local people. Dr. Goodall's mom's relationships with the local folk became the foundation for working together to find ways to

---

296 https://en.wikipedia.org/wiki/Ozone_depletion Accessed April 9, 2019

297 https://newenglandforestry.org/about/our-history/ Access April 22, 2019

protect the chimps while being sensitive to the needs of the people in the area.

Other amazing environmentalists include Carl Jones, who is credited with saving the Mauritius kestrel, the pink pigeon, the echo parakeet, and many other species from extinction.[298] Now that's a legacy! Greta Thunberg is a young climate activist who started sitting outside of the Swedish Parliament on Friday afternoons to protest their lack of action on climate change. Her protest has grown into an international phenomenon with hundreds of thousands of students demonstrating, striking from school, and demanding climate action in the Fridays for Future movement.

And then there are local heroes. I'm sure you know some in your community. I know many in mine. Jill organizes and works at countless community events, from sustainability talks, to the community market, as well as working on affordable housing projects, and co-counseling groups. Hannah and Clare have dramatically reduced their own homes' eco-footprints. They also run groups for toddlers in the local orchard, manage the flower beds on the village green, carry out biodiversity surveys, and volunteer for environmental actions in their village. Jenny picks up litter by the motorway service station, runs a village flower planting scheme, and volunteers tirelessly at her local church. Annie helps new gardeners learn, enriches all our lives and that of local wildlife with her beautiful organic garden, and is president of the local gardening club. Giles volunteers for various schemes around the village and down on the Somerset Levels to help wildlife thrive. The list could go on and on.

It may be that none of these local champions will spark international movements. We may never know the full impact we do have. Our greatest role may be indirect. We never know, one of our actions may be the drop which catalyzes reform and brings about social justice or the salvation of a species. Or our efforts may save a single pair of bluebirds or create a haven for dragonflies in our yard. Maybe our actions will spur a neighbor to

---

[298] https://www.theguardian.com/environment/2018/nov/26/its-very-easy-to-save-a-species-how-carl-jones-rescued-more-endangered-animals-than-anyone-else Accessed April 19, 2019

recycle, show others that we value local living, support a local farmer, or change a manufacturing method. But eco-conscious activities will certainly make our own lives more healthy. Even if no one sees it, whatever we choose to do, does matter. All our actions have impacts. Your voice, your actions, your choices all make a difference.

## Nature is resilient

### *Recovering Species.*

There are many examples of species that have come back from the edge of extinction. Perhaps most iconic is the very symbol of the USA: the bald eagle. In 1963 there were only 417 nesting pairs in the lower 48 states, but a recent count estimated more than 10,000 pairs. The majestic birds' recovery is due to both habitat protection and a ban on DDT, which makes the birds sterile and weakens any eggs which are produced.[299] Quite appropriately, the bald eagle is also sacred to some Native American groups, for the messages it carries between people and the gods. What message was our decimation of bald eagle populations carrying?

### *Wilding.*

Farming is a hard business and, sadly, often has a tiny financial profit. One family of farmers in West Sussex, England, realized that their dairy farm was close to bankruptcy while still being a tremendous amount of work. They decided to take advantage of government initiatives to protect and create wilderness and they let their farm go wild. Almost 20 years on and the wilderness at Knepp is lauded as an outstanding ecosystem restoration success. Over 400 species are on site, including extremely rare butterflies and plants, five species of owl, 62 species of bees, 30 species of wasps, peregrine falcons, and turtle doves. And financially, the wilderness seems to be making a go of it through a combination of subsidies, tourism, and meat sales from the culling of reintroduced grazers. The grazers were

[299] https://en.wikipedia.org/wiki/Bald_eagle Accessed April 22, 2019

introduced to keep the ecosystem in balance, and culling was needed as there were no natural predators, thus providing a handy sustainable meat source.[300] One estimate of the estate's income posted online states that Knepp farm earns £133 per acre, £21 higher than the average of other estates studied.[301] The book Wilding, about Knepp, makes for stimulating and uplifting reading and discusses how our ideas of ecosystem succession and the role of grazers have been readjusted following the documentation of Knepp's rewilding.[302]

## *Ham Wall and the Avalon Marshes.*

About 30 miles south of Bristol, in the southwest of England, is an area called the Somerset Levels. The Somerset Levels may be known to history buffs or Bernard Cromwell fans as the place where King Alfred hid and recovered his strength after a defeat by the Danes. Long ago, this area was a marsh and peatland. But historic and modernized peat extraction has changed the landscape dramatically. Many previously abundant species are no longer residents. The loss of the native peatland, which absorbed vast amounts of water and carbon, contributed to the financially devastating floods of 2013-2014.[303] In one pocket of this artificially drained landscape, a group of nature conservation bodies and private individuals have cobbled together a mosaic of new wetland habitats covering over five square miles. The restored wetland has quickly become a haven to internationally rare bird species. In particular, a pair of great bitterns bred in the reserve in 2008, making it the first time in 39 years that bitterns had bred in Somerset. Now, there are dozens of breeding pairs there. Other successes include resident otters, dragonflies, and great crested newts. As with Knepp Farm, the stewards have found an income stream via the restored ecosystem. In order to

---

[300] Tree, I. 2018, Wilding, Picador Publishers, London

[301] Attkinson, J. https://www.reaseheath.ac.uk/rewilding-knepp-creating-a-mess/ Accessed April 24, 2019

[302] Tree, I. 2018, Wilding, Picador Publishers, London

[303] https://en.wikipedia.org/wiki/Winter_flooding_of_2013%E2%80%9314_on_the_Somerset_Levels Accessed April 19, 2019

prevent the wetland being overgrown with reeds and becoming a grassland, volunteers remove the reeds. The reeds are then composted and sold to happy local gardeners who get a nutrient-rich soil improver with no weeds.[304]

Another exciting rewilding project is that of the Brooklyn Bridge Gardens. On 85 acres worth of paved over abandoned docks, in the center of New York City, are now 85 acres of greenspaces. Some have been converted to sports pitches and some to wilderness. In the 12 years since the start of construction, rare and endangered species have come to thrive in this city-based greenspace. For instance, the rare two-spotted ladybug has been seen there.[305] Indeed, green spaces in cities turn out to be critical habitats for many of our insect species and migrating birds.

## *Adaptable.*

Life is highly adaptable. Those species, or strains of species, which can take advantage of new conditions thrive. The changes which humanity is making to natural resources have an impact on which species thrive. One recent example of this is bacteria that eat plastic. They were discovered in 2016 at a waste dump in Japan. This could be good news for the plastic pollution problem, though many questions remain about the conditions needed for the bacteria to live and the effects it may have.[306] But what is clear is that it would be tough to kill off all life on the planet. Any individual being will strive to survive in the situation into which it is born. Think about trees that grow on cliffs. The unfathomable diversity of life means something is likely to survive and even thrive in most environments. Somehow this cheers me. Guess my bar is pretty low.

---

[304] RSPB Ham Wall National Nature Reserve Handout 2019 and personal communication with Giles Morris, biologist and long term volunteer at the site, April 19, 2019

[305] https://en.wikipedia.org/wiki/Brooklyn_Bridge_Park#Empire-Fulton_Ferry accessed March 9, 2020

[306] Carrington, D. April 16, 2018, "Scientists accidentally create mutant enzyme which eats plastic bottles", The Guardian, https://www.theguardian.com/environment/2018/apr/16/scientists-accidentally-create-mutant-enzyme-that-eats-plastic-bottles

## Groups finding solutions

Lots and lots of people, organizations, businesses, and governments are thinking about and working towards solving natural resource depletion.

### *The United Nations Sustainable Goals*

The United Nations has many environmental research and outreach programs. In addition, the UN organizes many international treaties and conventions on environmental issues. Perhaps most relevant to this book are the 17 Sustainable Goals for the year 2030, which range from poverty eradication to clean drinking water. The 17 goals were adopted by the UN's General Assembly in 2015.

### *Countries*

There are a load of environmental treaties between nations. For instance, CITES is the Convention on International Trade in Endangered Species of Wild Fauna and Flora. One hundred eighty-three countries are parties to the convention, which includes rules for trade of some 35,000 species of animals.[307] CITES made trade in elephant ivory illegal back in 1989, leading to the reduction of the killing of wild elephants. Unfortunately, elephant numbers continue to plummet by 8% a year, primarily due to illegal trade. Only 350,000 savannah elephants survive in Africa today, down from 10,000,000 in the early 1900s. So while treaties like CITES are fantastic, enforcement is critical.[308]

### *Non-Profit Organizations Which Protect and Nourish the Natural World Abound*

Undoubtedly there is one that aligns with your values, perhaps one of these: The Nature Conservancy, The Audubon

---

[307] https://en.wikipedia.org/wiki/CITES Accessed April 15, 2019

[308] Steyn, P. 2016, August 31, , "African elephant numbers plummet 30 percent, landmark survey finds", National Geographic, https://news.nationalgeographic.com/2016/08/wildlife-african-elephants-population-decrease-great-elephant-census/ Accessed April 17, 2019

Society, Natural Resource Defense Council, Marine Conservation Institute, International Fund for Animal Welfare, Global Footprint Network, Sierra Club, RSPB, or Defenders of Wildlife. If you seek a Christian angle to your eco-charity these are abundant as well including: A Rocha, Operation Noah, Christian Simple Living, Restoring Eden, Evangelical Environment Network, and Eco-Justice Ministries.

## Clever and doable solutions exist

There are loads of easy-to-implement practices in manufacturing, business, and running our homes to nurture the living world rather than harm it. As more and more of us demonstrate our support for greener activities, these will become standard practice. Often, all that is needed is an attitude change. Sometimes there will be a start-up cost, but this is almost always paid back in a short time. Humans are ingenious, and we can do amazing things when we put our minds to it. Here are a few innovations that are helping to nourish Earth's biosphere.

### *Conservation Agriculture*

A growing number of farmers are turning from traditional dig and plow farming methods to a focus on nurturing soil biodiversity. No-dig agriculture aims to disturb the soil column, and its phenomenally rich life, as little as possible. Compost is laid on top of the soil allowing creatures and physical processes, such as worms and the freeze/thaw cycle, to do the job of mixing nutrients into the soil. The immediate effect is a reduced running cost in terms of machinery, labor, pesticides, and fertilizers and an immediate increase in returns. But the real benefits appear a couple of years later when crop yields exceed previous years and profits are greater than ever. No-dig crops are more drought-resistant than on traditional dig farms as the soil organic matter increases, which can thus hold more water.[309] Aside from the financial and farming benefits, pesticide and fertilizer use is reduced and the healthier soils store vast amounts of greenhouse gases. No-dig planting is also gaining popularity in home gardening. Charles Dowding demonstrated that yields are higher and gardeners' backs much happier when one practices no-dig gardening.[310]

### *Modular Construction*

Modular buildings are 60-90% constructed off-site and transported to the location and put together. They can be made of wood, brick, or other materials and can look indistinguishable from on-site builds. However, modular construction buildings are recyclable! When the needs of a building shift, a modular structure can be rearranged or taken apart and used elsewhere. There are many environmental advantages to modular buildings, including far less waste of materials in both materials and packaging. Modular building results in less site damage during the build, and better temperature and damp insulation with higher indoor air quality in the final building. Furthermore, modular builds are less expensive and quicker to erect than onsite builds.[311]

### *Rewilding of the Biosphere*

An example of a multi-faceted winning plan is to re-establish destroyed forests and peatlands which are not currently farmed or built on. Reforestation creates more wilderness habitat, flood control, and water filtration, while stabilizing soils and removing vast amounts of greenhouse gases from the atmosphere.[312] If done sensitively, rewilding could also provide

---

[309] Taylor, M. 2019, " 'It's a groundswell': The farmers fighting to save the Earth's soil", published and accessed in The Guardian April 24, 2019, https://www.theguardian.com/world/2019/apr/24/farmers-save-earths-soil-conservation-agriculture

[310] Charles Dowding webpage https://www.charlesdowding.co.uk/ Accessed April 30, 2019

[311] Wikipedia page for "Modular Building", Accessed April 25, 2019 https://en.wikipedia.org/wiki/Modular_building

[312] Griscom, B.W. et al 2017, "Natural climate solutions", Proc. of the Nat. Acad. Sci. 114, 11645-11650.

resources for the world's most impoverished folk. What's not to like?

### *Driverless Cars*

Another amazing innovation that could solve a myriad of eco-problems are driverless cars, which are already being road-tested in Bristol, England, and elsewhere. If driverless cars can live up to their potential, they will reduce the cost of transport for everyone. Driverless cars have the potential to reduce the number of cars on our roads by a factor of 10, to free up urban space, to reduce emissions, and to reduce car-mortality rates by a factor of 10.[313]

### *Universal Credit*

Of course, some eco-solutions will require changing the shape of the labor market, driverless cars not least among them. At this point, we have to come to grips with the jobs versus the environment conflict. It is true, there would probably be job losses with the transition to a green economy. However, beyond five years or so a green economy will lead to a net increase in jobs. And it is not eco-conscious decisions that are primarily driving job losses today, but rather automation. The job market is *already* changing. Some eco-conscious choices will generate local, mom & pop shop type jobs or spur on green-technology jobs, but some will inevitably contribute to job losses as the economy changes. However, we can not forego natural resource protection for job protection. Quite simply, the planet's natural resources will not support everyone consuming the way we are now. One idea for coping with employment losses is universal basic income. The idea of universal income is not to replace work, but to enable folks to work part-time, to retrain, or to diversify their wealth streams.

Universal basic income takes a few different forms. However, the general idea is that every legal resident 18 and over receives a stipend each month from the government. This may sound far-fetched, but the concept is gaining traction in the US and around the world as automation has cut many traditional jobs

---

313 https://en.wikipedia.org/wiki/Self-driving_car#Potential_advantages Accessed April 9, 2019

and threatens many more. Andrew Yang, who ran for the 2020 Democratic presidential nomination, has suggested $1000 a month per person.[314] Universal basic income is also supported by the likes of Bill Gates, Mark Zuckerman, Elon Musk, and Sir Richard Branson.[315] Five countries have already run trials.[316] A guaranteed basic income would diversify our wealth portfolios too. With a reliable small income, folks would be able to explore homesteading, hobbies/careers, further education, or raise a family without having to risk extreme poverty. Of course, a national health service, as the UK has, would facilitate this.

## Awareness is growing

As someone who is a lifelong eco-advocate, I have noticed an enormous shift in public awareness concerning environmental issues. I can recall the eye-rolling from family and friends when I mentioned the hot topics of the 70s and 80s: recycling, contrails, or rainforest destruction. While I still get the occasional shirk off, the response of most people couldn't be more different. For example, it seems as if the overuse of plastics went from a marginal issue discussed by fringe groups of surfers and crazy ladies who pick up garbage on the beach (self included) to broad public demand for change in the last year or two.

We've seen a shift in the past two years on other issues as well, especially the great good we can do by reducing our meat intake. Previously, many of us were aware that factory-reared livestock live in dreadful conditions. But now, it is almost universally recognized that the livestock industry is a major driver in the loss of habitat and biodiversity, soil degradation, oceanic damage, and freshwater health. And the acceptance that climate change is driven by humanity is rising too. Seventy percent of

---

[314] https://www.yang2020.com/ Accessed April 12, 2019

[315] https://www.thebalance.com/universal-basic-income-4160668 Accessed April 12, 2019

[316] https://www.worldcrunch.com/culture-society/universal-basic-income-5-experiments-from-around-the-world-1 Accessed April 12, 2019

Americans now think global warming is happening, an increase of 7% between 2013 and 2016.[317]

And with an acknowledged awareness of the problems, the sky's the limit. Whereas, if we don't fix the problems in the sky, our lives will be limited. But also if we bear down and acknowledge the problem, the potential innovations are limitless. If we don't believe there is a problem, we won't change how we spend our money or vote. Acceptance that there is an environmental crisis, is not just half the battle, it is THE critical battle. So get out there and talk about it, even if you're not convinced - then talk about that. Thank you.

## Mobilizing for change

A final note on the hopefulness of the current times comes from the work of Erica Chenoweth and Maria Stephan. Their work shows that non-violent campaigns for change have been very successful in the last 100 years. Non-violent campaigns are twice as likely to succeed as violent protests, and they promote durable and peaceful solutions. Perhaps the most famous example of a successful nonviolent campaign is Gandhi's movement which led to India's independence from Britain. Change in governments or policies has been found to arise when 3.5% of the population was mobilized.[318] I think we are nearing the threshold of participation needed to spur our governments and industries to start prioritizing our natural resources and our long-term well-being.

## Moving forward

It's important to remember that making eco-conscious choices is not a sacrifice but rather a wealth of opportunities. Just

---

[317] Leiserowitz, A., Maibach, E., Roser-Renouf, C., Rosenthal, S., Cutler, M., & Kotcher, J. (2018). *Climate change in the American mind: March 2018.* Yale University and George Mason University. New Haven, CT: Yale Program on Climate Change Communication.

[318] Chenoweth, E. and M. J. Stephan, 2011. *Why Civil Resistance Works: The Strategic Logic of Nonviolent Conflict*, New York, NY: Columbia University Press.

like choosing to eat a well-balanced meal is good for us in many ways, eco-conscious choices also yield multiple rewards including economic, political, and social benefits , as well as environmental benefits. And not just for ourselves, for green choices impact up and down the social scale from individuals to governments, and then back down again to individuals. In addition, helping our household or community to address eco-issues empowers us, connects us with others, and gives us meaning and purpose. We need you, whatever your level of commitment. Everyone's contribution to protecting nature is vital whether we frame it as working for other people, other times, or other species. Working for others: is this not the greatest work of all?

# Epilogue

As I've finished writing this book, we are going through the coronavirus pandemic. I can't help but see countless parallels with how this situation is unfolding and how we are handling environmental issues.

For years, experts have warned us that we should prepare, materially and knowledge-wise, for coming pandemics. Not least because climate change is increasing the ranges of malaria and other infectious diseases. Then in January, 2020, China erupted in CoVID 19. The US could have quickly accelerated preparations for dealing with this disease at that point. However, the Center for Global Pandemics had been shut by the current US administration as part of a 15 billion dollar cut to health care programs under Trump. Instead of making and distributing test kits, planning how to protect health care workers, and supporting those who had to stay home, the government's approach during January and February was to claim the danger of the virus was a left-wing conspiracy. We should all keep working and keep consuming.

While we are only beginning to see the impacts of CoVID, we need to think about how we want to continue as a culture. Business-as-usual is a bad plan. It is a driving-off-a-cliff-with-a-blindfold-on plan. The need to kickstart our economies back into gear following this crisis is a unique opportunity to change our course. Why don't we invest in a New Deal like work program which develops green technology? Why not recenter our military might into well-being fortitude? Rest assured that the corporate world is in action to take advantage of this chaos.

If you've ever read Naomi Klein's *Shock and Awe*, you'll be aware that the US government has repeatedly and intentionally frothed up unrest in other countries in order that the US might swoop in with US corporate centric economic plans to 'save the day'. This is happening domestically during the current crisis, with roll backs of environmental regulations including drastic weakening of the century-old Migratory Bird Treaty Act, elimination of vehicle emission restrictions (really? Don't you want clean air right now so your lungs stay healthy?), and facilitating development at the Chaco Culture World Heritage site and an Alaskan wilderness. All these rollbacks in concert with reducing the public comment period from 60 days to 30 threatens to squeeze these things through before we have a chance to even comment on them. We, champions of the good life, need to be alert and active too. How do we do this? How we vote is critical. Campaign and lobbying laws need to be changed so we return to democracy. Let's vote and campaign for a world where the public's opinion matters more to policy than corporations' opinions. Meanwhile, if you're so minded, you can sign up for alerts with various watchdogs and let your senators and representatives know what you think.

Another parallel between environmental depletion and the Covid-19 pandemic is that the poor are hit disproportionally hard by both. And, again, in both cases this arises from underlying conditions, lack of monetary resources to cushion blows, and less access to health care, all while living / working on the frontlines. During this crisis, residents in counties in the US with a majority of black residents are three times as likely to contract the virus and six times more likely to die from it relative to residents in majority white counties.[319] Those in low-paying jobs are less likely to be able to work remotely, to have paid sick leave, and to have a financial cushion. Many are faced with the choice of going to work and interacting with the public or protecting their health and quitting their jobs. If they are so unfortunate as to live in the United States, quitting their job will also mean losing their health insurance. It is a no-win situation for many families.

But it is not all gloom and doom. Many positives are coming out of this crisis. We have been reminded that we are all interconnected. My virus soon becomes yours and our extended

[319] Scott, E., April 10, 2020, "4 reasons coronavirus is hitting black communities so hard", The Washington Post, Accessed May 5, 2020, https://www.washingtonpost.com/politics/2020/04/10/4-reasons-coronavirus-is-hitting-black-communities-so-hard/

circles reach across the world. And we are also seeing that we have far more in common than that which divides us. And people are being great. From helpful neighbors to volunteers right up to the heroic health care workers and grocery store clerks. And we've not just been reminded that humanity is one big family, we've been forced to acknowledge that we are part of nature. The likely transfer of Covid-19 from bats to humans was facilitated by deforestation and the sale of wild animals. Covid-19 is the third such virus thought to have made this journey in the last few decades, following in the footsteps of SARS and MERS. It is estimated that at least 330 emerging infectious diseases since 1930 came from our consumption of wilderness.[320] In addition, scientists have identified some 30,000 corona viruses in animals which become more likely to jump to humans as we continue to cut into the existing habitats of wild animals and expose ourselves to their diseases.[321] Maybe we ought to stop cutting into the life of the planet?

Other positives have been the stunningly good air quality in various cities. For example, in Delhi the Air Quality Index, which is deemed safe at levels below 25, regularly sits around 200 on a good pre-Covid day. Sometimes it even exceeds 900. But now the Air Quality Index has fallen below 20. Clean blue skies, views of mountains obscured for decades and non-deadly air.[322] That seems priceless to me. The canals in Venice have transformed

---

[320] Berkley, S., Feb 4, 2020, "Novel Coronavirus is a Reminder: The Best Defense against a New Viral Outbreak is Early Detection", Scientific American, https://blogs.scientificamerican.com/observations/novel-coronavirus-is-a-reminder-the-best-defense-against-a-new-viral-outbreak-is-early-detection/, accessed April 17, 2020

[321] McMahon, J., April 1, 2020 "Deforestation and climate change could unleash mind-boggling number of coronaviruses", Forbes, https://www.forbes.com/sites/jeffmcmahon/2020/04/01/there-are-30000-more-coronaviruses-environmental-disasters-are-bringing-them-to-your-door/#4a49ca9e85c8, accessed April 17, 2020

[322] Ellis-Peterson, H.E. et al, April 11, 2020, "It's positively alpine: Disbelief in big cities as air pollution falls", The Guardian, Accessed April 17, 2020 https://www.theguardian.com/environment/2020/apr/11/positively-alpine-disbelief-air-pollution-falls-lockdown-coronavirus?utm_term=RWRpdG9yaWFsX0dyZWVuTGlnaHQtMjAwNDE1&utm_source=esp&utm_medium=Email&CMP=greenlight_email&utm_campaign=GreenLight

from murky, polluted, stinky water into clear blue ecosystems in which wildlife is now seen.[323] Again, priceless. These inspiring transformations are being repeated across the globe. In my own garden, which backs onto a major road and is under a flight path, engine noise and emissions are much lower making the birdsong louder and the skies bluer.

We also have the bonus of families spending more time together. Sometimes not so easy, granted, but we are reminded of what really matters. Can we take these positives forward? Perhaps our new normal will include far fewer car journeys and fewer shopping trips. Less stuff and more connections. And as to economic worries, analyses have shown that a green stimulus package will create more jobs in the short and long term than conventional spending or the bailout strategy following the financial crisis of 2008.[324] We are at a crux point in our history. Will we choose back to normal or take the opportunity to make our society greener, more equitable, just and long lived.

As I make the final edits on this book, we've all localized our lives a great deal because of COVID. We've found creative solutions to work and play, saving vast amounts of time, energy and money. As well as reducing our carbon emissions, this hermitic lifestyle, has vastly reduced my 'to do' list. While the isolation is oppressive at times, I find the quiet aspects of our new lifestyles liberating. Of course, we all hope we can visit with one another more freely very soon, but I trust we will take forward some of the lessons we've learned. In addition to the personal lessons of 'what really matters' and so forth, society as a whole has adjusted quite quickly and become more accepting of different modes of work - it's no longer shocking if the dog barks in the midst of a phone call or a toddler wanders through the background. Change can be initially difficult, but often it is easier than imagined and more beneficial than we could have anticipated.

---

[323] Brunton, J. March 20, 2020, " 'Nature is taking back Venice': wildlife returns to tourist free city" The Guardian, Accessed April 17, 2020, https://www.theguardian.com/environment/2020/mar/20/nature-is-taking-back-venice-wildlife-returns-to-tourist-free-city

[324] Harvy, F. May 5, 2020, Green stimulus can repair global economy and climate, says study", The Guardian

## *Epilogue*

In summary, the Covid-19 pandemic has had the following responses from society: expert warnings of such an event for decades previously, scientific understanding of the problems and solutions, signs of an impending disaster, the ignoring of expert advice even as the crisis took hold, the spread of misinformation, weak preparation, a disproportionate impact on the poor, and the distortion of research for political ends.

The impact of COVID-19 and the lives lost are the baby sister of what will happen if we don't significantly alter how we consume. Hopefully we can take this wake-up call and move towards a less capitalistic society where non-monetary wealth is valued, such as natural capital, well-being capital, social capital, and skills and knowledge capital. Perhaps we could see a reinvigoration of our local village's economy. Ideally, we will use the economic stimulus packages of 2020 to kickstart a green technology revolution. I hope we do. But we won't unless we all get out there, or stay in here, and make positive changes with our votes, our money, and our voices. Respectfully. Kindly. Powerfully. Peace be with you.

# ABOUT THE AUTHOR

Prudence Foster has spent over 30 years doing scientific research. Her studies range across a broad array of fields always searching for underlying causes of natural phenomena. With a Ph.D. in astrophysics, she has used numerical techniques to tease out fundamental mechanisms in the global carbon cycle, impacts of climate change on ecosystems, and star formation. She has held posts at the University of Bristol, England, the University of Tokyo and the Carnegie Institution of Washington. Dr. Foster is also a longterm environmental advocate and has long worked to make the world a more vibrant place for people and other species. Her environmental advocacy has included work with the Great Ape Project, community gardening and sustainability, public engagement, and communication. She believes that all individuals are inherently valuable, deserve respect, and have something to teach each of us.


# ACKNOWLEDGMENTS

Thanks to my wonderful sisters, Nedra and Ann, who not only enrich my life, but also edited and designed the cover for this book. And also much appreciation to Maxwell van Dyck - an inspiring young man who designed the chapter title artwork. Thanks to Connie, one of my lifelong best mates who was my first reader and always provides excellent insight and support. Thanks to the extended Walter and Foster clan, gardening buddies, and friends far and wide for your support with this book and all my mad endeavors.

Made in the USA
Middletown, DE
25 October 2020

22751036R00106